JOHNNY UNITAS

MISTER QUARTERBACK

JOHNNY UNITAS

MISTER QUARTERBACK

MIKE TOWLE

Cumberland House
Nashville, Tennessee

Copyright © 2003 by Michael J. Towle

Published by
Cumberland House Publishing, Inc.
431 Harding Industrial Drive
Nashville, TN 37211-3160

Cover design: Gore Studio, Inc.
Text design: John Mitchell

Library of Congress Cataloging-in-Publication Data

Towle, Mike.
  Johnny Unitas : mister quarterback / Mike Towle.
     p. cm.
Includes bibliographical references and index.
  ISBN 1-58182-361-4 (pbk. : alk. paper)
  1.   Unitas, Johnny, 1933- 2.   Football   players—United   States—Biography.
I. Title.
  GV939.U5T69 2003
  796.332'092—dc22

                                              2003017811

Printed in Canada
1 2 3 4 5 6 7—09 08 07 06 05 04 03

CONTENTS

To Mom and Dad. My parents celebrated their fiftieth wedding anniversary and my dad his eightieth birthday around the time this book was being written.
I love and cherish them both.

Acknowledgments

Getting people to consent to an interview for this book, let alone getting them to open up, is nothing an inquiring mind takes for granted. I thank the following for their accessibility: Ernie Accorsi, Tom Armstrong, Raymond Berry, Hal Bethea, Reggie Bethea, Ray Brown, LoAnn Dellis, Michael Dellis, Ray Farmer, Walter Fightmaster, Frank Gitschier, Ralph Green, Shirley Green, Alex Hawkins, Sam Huff, Jim "Moe" Laitta, Lenny Lyles, Tom Matte, Michael McDonald, Lenny Moore, Andy Nelson, Frank Otte, Ron Petrelli, Rosemary Rausch, Chuck "Bear" Rogers, Richard Sammis, Joe Trabue, Clark Wood, and Fred Zangaro. Some of those folks also were willing to part for a while with a photo or two to be used in this book, and their generosity, and trust, are much appreciated.

Frank Gitschier spent the better part of an entire afternoon with me, not only sharing his thoughts and memories of his good friend Johnny Unitas but also giving me a guided tour of the football memorabilia room and the Unitas statue at the University of Louisville. Kenny Klein, Andy Knapick, and the entire U of L sports information office rolled out the red carpet in opening up their archives. Photographer Dave Klotz made photo research a snap. Thanks also to the public relations staffs of the Indianapolis Colts and San Diego Chargers for helping me in my research.

One benefit of doing this book was, in the course of conducting interviews, getting the chance to eat at two of the finest dining establishments in Timonium, Maryland, north of Baltimore—Michael's Café, owned by Unitas friends Michael and LoAnn Dellis, and Andy Nelson's Southern Pit Barbecue, run by former Colts teammate Andy Nelson. These are not paid endorsements, merely an unsolicited thumbs-up to wonderful eating experiences, paid for by the author.

Kudos once again to the fine folks at Cumberland House for their faith and support in this project, as well as numerous others. Ron Pitkin, John Mitchell, Ed Curtis, Julie Jayne, Stacie Bauerle, and Gabby Benson are friends as well as helpers.

To my wife, Holley, and son, Andrew: They frequently thank me for putting in the work and long hours to author these books, but their sacrifices are every bit as important in making this possible. I couldn't ask for two people more supportive of what I do, and with no strings attached. I love you both.

Finally, a life without Jesus Christ in my heart and in my corner would be an empty one. Thank God for His Son's salvation, a deal that's good for eternity and available for anyone.

INTRODUCTION

John Unitas was classic old school. He kept the buzz cut well into his thirties, regularly attended Mass, played through pain without whimpering, and he took his black hightops home with him after playing his last game with the Baltimore Colts. He worked after (and before) school to make money to help support his family, and he never griped about the bad hand dealt his family when his dad died young.

When it came to football, the team was his thing, not individual achievements or statistics. He didn't suffer foolish backtalk in the huddle, and he didn't send his agent to negotiate when his coach asked him to stay after practice for an extra fifteen minutes of work. Usually, Unitas was the one asking his centers or receivers to stay with him after practice, not the coach.

Nothing came easy for Unitas. He had to work for everything. Schoolwork was something of a grind for him. At times, football was too. A natural athlete, he had a good arm and great field vision, but he wasn't particularly fast, and he was skinny all through his adolescence. It wasn't easy for him to get noticed. Unitas played at a small Catholic high school, and college coaches didn't know anything about him. Then he played at a relatively unknown college that drastically de-emphasized its football program a year after he arrived. Most pro scouts didn't go after Unitas because they didn't know they were supposed to be looking for him.

Thanks to his Louisville coaches networking on his behalf as well as they could, Unitas was selected in the ninth round of the 1955 National Football League draft by the Pittsburgh Steelers, but it was a wasted pick. The Steelers had three other quarterbacks in line ahead of Unitas, and they pretty much ignored the rookie in training camp—until it came time to make cuts.

Justice would have been served had Unitas gotten a chance to author *Football for Dummies*—his chapter on the Steelers would have been a hoot. He could have added a sidebar on the Cleveland Browns: Head coach Paul Brown was well-acquainted with Louisville head coach Frank Camp, but he ignored Camp's pleadings to take a flyer on Unitas.

Bully for the Baltimore Colts, who gave Unitas a legitimate tryout in 1956. Not only did he make the team, he became their starter a third of the way into the season, and in 1958 and 1959 he led the Colts to the NFL Championship. Unitas would end up spending seventeen years with the Colts before reluctantly finishing his career with the San Diego Chargers in 1973, an awkward and anticlimactic swan song about as out of kilter as Babe Ruth's final days with the Boston Braves, or Yogi Berra giving it one last go with the hapless New York Mets.

Unitas passed away, suddenly, on September 11, 2002, on the first anniversary of the terrorist attacks on the United States and about eight months short of what would have been his seventieth birthday. He left us knowing that he had been selected as the Greatest Player in the First Fifty Years of Pro Football, although he would never have admitted to such an honor unsolicited. Visitors to the Unitas household looking to view a personal shrine of awards and trophies would have been disappointed; most were stashed away in basement cabinets.

Let's get John Unitas, his exploits, and his life out into the open, thanks to the dozens of friends, acquaintances, peers, and former teammates who speak openly about this common man with the uncommon touch.

JOHNNY UNITAS

MISTER QUARTERBACK

1

STEEL TOWN

John Unitas was a terrific high school quarterback living in the outskirts of the big city, but he was a nobody. At best, he was agate type in the Pittsburgh papers. At worst, he was the accident-prone kid shoveling tons of coal by age eight to help support his fatherless family.

The folks in the Mount Washington neighborhood knew who he was, even if the rest of Pittsburgh didn't. He was scrappy but scrawny, a rocket-armed phenom who could rifle jump-passes deep downfield. Yet school nuns sent notes home asking John's overworked, widowed mom why she was apparently starving her children.

Five of the greatest quarterbacks in history came out of western Pennsylvania, and all but one fit the profile of big-time quarterback. There's "Broadway" Joe Namath, who predicted a major Super Bowl upset and then delivered to secure his place in celebrityhood; Joe Montana, who was gangly but went gangbusters once he got his shot at Notre

Dame before going on to lead the San Francisco Forty-niners to four Super Bowl titles; Dan Marino, the consummate drop-back passer with the Hollywood looks who aced *Ace Ventura: Pet Detective*; and Jim Kelly, the strapping USFL prodigy who would eventually take the Buffalo Bills to several Super Bowls.

Then there was Unitas, the flattopped, hightopped, stoop-shouldered, skinny-legged kid who could have spent his adult life in a coal mine and no one would have blinked. As it turned out, though, Johnny had 'em all beat. But for the longest time, Johnny, we hardly knew ye.

SHIRLEY "TOOTS" GREEN was one of Leon and Helen Unitas's four children, and Johnny's younger sister by a year and a half. She remembers growing up in the greater Pittsburgh area with an ironwoman mom whose work ethic rubbed off on all her kids:

Our father passed away when we were young. My mom didn't have enough money to maintain the house we lived in, so we had to move from Brookline to Mount Washington. Our new house had only two bedrooms, and we had four kids—my sister, Millie; my brothers, Leonard and John; and myself. Then there was my mom and a great-uncle with miner's asthma who lived with us. He couldn't work, so he would be at the house when we came home from school.

My mom cleaned offices, worked in a bakery, and sold insurance, and all that pretty much overlapped. We didn't have any insurance, and back then there was no social security. So whatever she could provide, that's what we lived on. A lot of times she couldn't be home for dinner. That was when she was out selling insurance. She worked in an area called Chicken Hills, which was comprised of a bunch of hills all over Mount Washington. These were those old insurance policies with premiums that were like five cents a week, short-term policies, and she had to walk doing all this. Mom would have to go out every other week to collect the money from these folks.

At the same time, she was going to night school to learn to be a bookkeeper. She was an incredible person, very, very strong. She wasn't a real affectionate person, and she had to work really hard to put bread on the table. Every morning, she would leave a list for us on the table telling us what needed to be done, because she would be gone almost all of the time. She would write down all these things that each person had to do, and you were scared to death not to do them. She was usually gone before we got up in the morning to go to school.

Leonard, the oldest, was about twelve when our father passed away; Millie was nine, John six, and me four. When we were growing up, Leonard was my father figure. I went to him rather than my mom for any kind of problem I had. We didn't want to cause Mom any more headaches than she already had.

Leonard didn't really have much of a childhood. He sold papers, and when he was old enough to drive, he drove a coal truck and delivered coal. He would do this early in the morning before going to school, when he was in high school. He would have to get up at about four in the morning and then go wait in line to get coal delivered into his truck.

The other three of us would have to do all the stuff around the house, like cleaning and laundry. We all worked together at it. We had a coal furnace, and John used to have to take care of it so that it would still be on when we got home after school in the afternoon. On Saturdays I would clean the ashes out from the stove and John would help Leonard with his coal deliveries. That's what our life was like: You got up in the morning and just did what needed to be done.

Because Shirley and John were the two youngest kids and fairly close in age, they had a fairly good bond, even though John certainly was not the outgoing one. What he was, however, was accident-prone. Even when John was an All-Pro quarterback, she would wince at some of the things she saw happen to her brother.
SHIRLEY GREEN:

When he got hurt, my stomach would just drop. Such as when he got the punctured lung—you just didn't know if he was going to be all right, if he was even going to get back up again. He ended up with a lot of scars, and that part of it hurt, seeing him like that.

He was the type of guy who never shied away from the kind of plays in which he might get hurt. He was like that as a kid, too. The one incident I remember the most was the time he shot himself in the hand, by accident.

Our house was kind of remote, near the woods. We had had a prowler around in the neighborhood, so one of my mother's brothers brought a gun over to keep in the house, for protection. He had put it on a mantel. One day John and I were home alone. He was about fifteen or sixteen. I was upstairs cleaning. Apparently, he got the gun and emptied the bullets but forgot that there was one in the chamber. He pulled the trigger, and I heard a *Pop!* I ran downstairs, and he was just standing there, blood everywhere. I looked at him and said, "What did you do?" And he said, "I shot myself." But he wasn't yelling or screaming—he was as calm as could be.

I got a towel and wrapped his hand in it. There was a doctor on Bailey Avenue, and John and I ran through the woods and up a hill to get to his house, which was about five minutes away. When the doctor saw that it was a gunshot, he wouldn't touch John. He told us we needed to take him to the hospital. Meanwhile, he's still bleeding all over the place.

This doctor would not do anything. So there we were, a couple of scared teenagers, too frightened to plead our case. When the doctor told us to leave, we just left.

PHOTO COURTESY OF SHIRLEY GREEN

John, at age twelve, with his pal Skippy.

I was really concerned that John was going to bleed to death, yet he said nothing the whole time. Absolutely nothing—he didn't even talk, even though he must have been in terrible pain, at least in shock. When we were at the doctor's house, I did all the talking. I didn't know what else to do, and there were no other adults around. My older sister had moved away from home, and that great-uncle of ours had passed away by then.

So we ran back down the hill and back through the woods. We had neighbors, very few of whom had cars. But there was one man we knew and he had a car, so I ran over to his house and knocked on the door. Thankfully, he got us into his car and drove us to the local hospital. As soon as we got down there, they called the police right away. They also called my mom at work. The police came to our house and took the gun. They kept thinking that I had shot John.

John was treated at the hospital, and they put a splint on his hand. We then went home, although that was the end of having any guns in our house. Over the years, the shooting would come up in discussion some times, but we never talked a whole lot about it ever again. I think it was something he wanted to forget.

As **SHIRLEY GREEN** *points out, this was not the first time that young John had had a mishap with a firearm:*

This was a few years earlier and involved a BB gun that Leonard owned. John, about seven, somehow got ahold of a cartridge, I think from a 30.06. He stuck the cartridge into a log out behind our house and then started shooting at it with the BB gun, trying to detonate the cartridge.

When the cartridge exploded, some shrapnel went into his left leg, in a spot where doctors couldn't remove it. So that's where it stayed, in his leg, until he died. Removing all of the lodged shrapnel would have meant damaging some muscles, although they were able to get some of it out.

John *was* accident-prone. My mom used to say that he couldn't walk and chew gum at the same time. But, boy, was he a tough guy. We all were, mostly because my mom didn't want to hear about these things. You just toughed things out and didn't talk about it, and crying was pretty much unacceptable.

The only times I ever saw John cry was when Ralph and I lost a son, Scott, who was twenty-nine when he died of cancer in 1989. John drove all night to be there with me and we just sobbed all night. Then our mom died the very next year, in 1990. Those were the only two times I ever saw John break down and cry.

Some people say that John was cold. Not to me. I think he would have given me anything I wanted. I never asked him for anything, but I know he would have come through if I had asked. We had a good relationship. He wasn't a soft person, but his love of children was unreal. He was so wonderful with our five boys. When he would come to visit, he paid a lot of attention to them—he was a wonderful uncle.

SHIRLEY offers some more insight on young John's character and their family's dynamics:

John was extremely quiet. He never had very much to say. Leonard and I were a bit more animated, although Millie was quiet, too. She was a sweet girl, and sometimes Leonard and I took advantage of her a little bit.

One thing John seemed to have a knack for was being able to make you mad, but he would never fight. For example, you might try to carry on a conversation with him about something, and he wouldn't enter into it. Or, you might try to tell him something and he would sort of ignore it, and that would make me mad. I used to throw things at him, but you could never get him to blow a gasket. He would just leave the room.

In the summertime, we would go to a nearby high school with a summer program that offered activities such as baseball, basketball, and swimming. They had an indoor swimming pool, but you wouldn't find John in it. He wasn't a water person at all. Even as he got older, he had a healthy fear of water. He played everything else and was always really good at whatever he did.

In grade school, a Catholic school, he played basketball. He was an excellent player and was always playing with the older kids.

Terrific at basketball, all through high school as well, John's first love was football, by far. He was always

*looking for a way to make himself a better quarter-
back.* **SHIRLEY GREEN:**

At home, John tied a bullwhip on a big tree and hanged a
truck tire from it. I would stand by the tire and start swinging it back and forth, keeping it going, while he would stand
a ways away and throw the football through it. He was great
at doing it, and he would do this for hours.

Sure, I sometimes got tired of intermittently pushing the
tire to keep it swinging, but I really enjoyed doing it with
him. For one thing, he was such a good kid. He always did
what he was supposed to do and never caused my mom any
problems. Sometimes I would retrieve the ball for him, and
other times I would stand behind the tire if it was swinging
okay on its own and try to catch, or at least stop, as many of
the passes as I could.

In the summertime we played baseball right after dinner.
We would play in the street until it was a little bit dark. He
was an excellent pitcher. After that, all of the neighborhood
kids would play a game called Release, in which we would
break up into two groups; one group would run and hide,
and the other group had to come and find you. Those cap-
tured had to come back to a designated spot, although those
kids still hiding could sneak in and release imprisoned teammates. We also played Kick the Can. Johnny would play
with us, but a lot of times when he ran off to hide, he would
just keep going, get a pint of ice cream, and sit on the corner
eating it.

*Shirley Unitas would end up meeting and marrying
Ralph Green, a classmate of John's who played point
guard on the basketball team and halfback in football.*
RALPH GREEN:

I met John once we got to high school, and we became pretty good friends. We used to trade comic books while sitting on the porches of our houses on Williams Street. Batman and Superman were our favorites. It started with just Johnny and me, and then Toots (Shirley) would get involved. She was a snot-nosed little kid, the little sister that no one thinks about, but she grew up and eventually got my attention.

Another thing John and I did was hang out on street corners, eating a ton of ice cream. Those were the good ol' days of summertime.

***

RALPH GREEN *witnessed early on how John Unitas would play through pain:*

Not long after John had shot himself, his center finger was in a six-inch splint, wrapped in white tape. It was football season. I can picture him to this day, his finger sticking straight up, and him throwing the ball about fifty-five yards at Moon Township on a field that was like a cow pasture. It *was* a cow pasture, in fact, because there was some manure and other stuff out there. John could still wing that football, gunshot wound and all.

***

JIM "MOE" LAITTA *was another of John's pals and football teammates at Saint Justin's. Laitta was a center on offense and made first string his junior year:*

It was a very close-knit school. There was a spirit there that would be similar to what they have at the University of Notre Dame.

When it came to personality, John wasn't what you would call an outgoing guy. But when it came to athletics, he was really something else. After his dad died, his family moved to a house with a big lawn, right across the street from me. I used to buddy around with him and some of the other guys from high school.

John wasn't a guy you saw standing around with his hands in his pockets. He was a hardworking guy. He had to go out and make some money.

John always stayed in the background. He never beat his chest. He might have been the most humble guy I ever met. I have an eight-by-ten photo of our football team from high school, and there's John back there in the third row—you can barely make out his face. Same deal with a class picture, in which he is in the background, looking subdued. John was a serious person—he was private. He had to know he was good at football, but you would never know it by talking to him.

I remember tossing the football around with him in his yard, and he would throw the ball so hard it would knock me on my butt.

LAITTA continues, offering more background on Saint Justin's and playing football alongside Unitas:

We were a Class B school, and there were three schools in our area—us, Saint Mary's, and Saint George's. We had a pretty good rivalry between the three of us. We would play games at Moore Field in Brookline, and the place would be packed.

I can remember one game in which we had the ball inside our own ten-yard line, and it was fourth down. I was at center and John had dropped back a few steps to do the kicking and to try and get us out of there.

In the huddle, we agreed that the signal to hike the ball on was fifty-four. When I got over the ball, I kept repeating fifty-four to myself over and over to make sure I wouldn't forget it. I guess I was so focused on that, that I didn't hear John when he called out "Fifty-four!" He repeated it, and still I didn't hear him. Finally, he yelled, "Center the damn ball!"

I centered it, all right—beautifully, right over his head. It wasn't one of my sterling moments, but what I remember about it is that he never gave me a hard time about it or held it against me.

The coach would let John call the plays, and when he started to talk in the huddle, you just kept quiet. He was in charge. He was a general, even in high school.

John was poetry in motion—those stands were packed. He had a tremendous reputation, even in high school.

Academically, Unitas wasn't exactly poetic. **LAITTA:**

I took a lot of classes in high school with John. I can remember him in French class, standing up and trying to speak French. It didn't go so well. I started to laugh and he gave me the worst look. Not a pretty sight.

Unitas did read, however, as his sister **SHIRLEY GREEN** *points out:*

You couldn't help but see it: Every book he ever got out of the library was a book about a quarterback. He was always reading something like *The Sid Luckman Story*. All he wanted was football.[1]

Another of John's boyhood pals was **RON PETRELLI,** *who likewise grew up in the Mount Washington area of Pittsburgh:*

Johnny Unitas in high school, looking like a lean, mean, throwing machine.

I knew John from playing ball and hanging around on the street in the neighborhood. But he wasn't the kind of kid to hang there for a long time—he needed to get home. There weren't many one-parent families in those days, and I suppose he needed to get home because he had so many chores that needed to be done. He probably had to work more so than the rest of us.

Saint Justin's was a nice, small neighborhood parochial school. We probably had about 400 students in grade school and about 350 in high school. It wasn't large at all compared to the schools you hear about now, especially the combined schools. There was good community interplay between the schools, some of which were only about five or six blocks away from each other.

It was a tight community, and you knew everybody. You walked to school instead of taking a bus. You got to see and meet a lot of the guys you played against in sports.

PETRELLI *continues:*

John was a pretty good athlete all the way around. One thing John could do was throw one heckuva long ball. He used to try that jump pass, too. I think he even did it once or twice with Baltimore. In high school, he threw the jump pass left-handed a couple of times. He liked to win and would do anything to do it. He was capable of doing weird things that guys today wouldn't even think about, things that involved quick improvising to get the mission accomplished. Back on those days, we were allowed to do about anything we wanted, more or less. He was just a natural athlete.

We generally played our games on Fridays, occasionally on Saturdays. It was a big event for Mount Washington and the schools that we played. Most of our games were against schools within a five-mile radius of Mount Washington, so the interest and rivalries were there.

Johnstown Catholic was one school that used to beat up on us pretty good. They were about twice as big as we were, with an enrollment of about eight hundred students. I remember they had this one big kid who weighed 210 and played fullback, where the biggest guy we had on defense weighed around 200. This guy was like Bronko Nagurski to us. Hard man to bring down, and he popped a few of our guys pretty good.

JOE UNITAS, *a cousin:*

He was a phenomenon. People wanted to come see this skinny, bowlegged kid jump up in the air and throw the ball forty yards. Of course, he was jumping because he couldn't see over the linemen.[2]

SHIRLEY GREEN *weighs in with her perspective on life with John while both were in high school:*

It was a very strict school. John fit in well there.

I knew that John was a really good athlete while in high school, but there wasn't yet a sense of how great he would end up being someday. I was a cheerleader, so I went to all the games, both football and basketball. One thing about him is that in going to away games, he would not let me sit on the bus with anybody but him. I always knew he was watching out for me—even at parties. But he was subtle about it—I never felt like he was trying to intimidate or control me in any way. I always felt safe.

Back at the house, Mom had a huge garden, so John and I had to weed and hoe and all that good stuff. The garden was so huge that we couldn't finish all the hoeing and weeding in one day. She grew everything, and then we canned everything in the fall. That's what we lived on in the wintertime. Corn, tomatoes, beans, cucumbers, lettuce . . . she grew everything.

John took his time doing stuff. If I wanted to get things moving so I could get to playing quicker, I could probably do three rows to his one. He was more methodical about everything. I don't think gardening was his favorite thing as a kid, but when he got older later on in life, he loved to garden. He loved flowers and loved working with the soil. All four of us are that way still.

John also loved riding around on a lawn tractor cutting the grass. He just loved being outside. That was solitude for him.

RALPH GREEN *got a sense of John's religious devotion while both were in high school:*

John was good at anything athletic, just a natural. One of the things that stands out in my mind is that we would get dressed for an away game and go get our equipment before getting on the bus, and no matter what day it was or what time it was, John would first go to church. Most of the team would follow him.

*If Mass was one of young John's biggest interests, casual conversation and girls were not. **SHIRLEY GREEN**:*

You could sit in a room with John for six hours, and you might get a word here or there. He was like a Gary Cooper, not a conversationalist. Didn't want any part of girls. He was a late bloomer in that regard.[3]

__SHIRLEY GREEN__, again:

One time the nuns (from school) called the house wondering if John and I were malnourished; that's how bad it was. My mother got really mad about that. There was always food on the table. We were just built like that.[4]

*Back to football, and **RON PETRELLI**, who was a running back on offense and a safety on defense, both of which kept him pretty close to Unitas:*

John would be right behind me on defense, always pushing me here or there to get in position for the play, and that's okay because he was the captain. He would also give you a shout telling you where to go. If he didn't lead you vocally, he wasn't averse to doing it physically, and he really knew what he was doing because he understood the game so well. You didn't pick and choose—he did it for you.

We ran a T on offense, not a single wing. We ran the T because of his abilities. We threw more than we ran, as I recall, and we had some decent receivers. He threw enough passes that it got him a look-see from Notre Dame. The two men who coached us had various connections, and that pretty much determined which colleges, if any, would know about us. That's why there weren't a lot of schools coming after John—not many knew about him. It was easy in those days for any player to fall below the radar.

John was very big in this area, but outside the area I doubt if anyone knew him. He was never all-city or anything like that. We were small potatoes. We were lucky if we could field an entire offense and defense with a half-dozen guys left over, what we called "recruits."

One of the schools that eventually came calling on John Unitas was the University of Louisville. Cardinals assistant coach **FRANK GITSCHIER,** *who had recently completed a quarterbacking stint at the school, had been turned on to Unitas by two former Pittsburgh-area players who were playing at Louisville. Gitschier:*

When I recruited John at his home in Mount Washington, with the two Louisville players in tow, I saw a sack of coal lying there in front of the house. Right away, I knew I would be able to communicate with him and his family. I knew where he was coming from.

I felt real encouraged, because I could remember being a kid (in Sharon, Pennsylvania) and my dad sending me down to the coal yard to get a big bag of coal that weighed about fifty pounds. I couldn't pick it up, so I would drag it home. The sack was light burlap and it would tear open, and as soon as I got the bag home, I would run back down the street and pick up all the pieces that had fallen out and put them in the bag before my dad found out and whipped me.

Helen Unitas had a great effect on John's life. This might not be an exact quote, but I remember her saying, "Don't tell me what you want; you tell me what you need."

GITSCHIER, who would forge a relationship with Unitas that lasted fifty-two years, not only had to recruit John, he had to sell himself and Louisville to John's mom, Helen. Gitschier gives some background on how and why he ended up trekking to Mount Washington in the first place:

I was coaching at the University of Louisville. Coach Joe Trabue and I were coaching the freshmen from one to two-thirty, then we would get a drink in the bathroom and go to the coaches meeting. At one of those meetings, (head coach Frank Camp) said, "We need a center and a quarterback next year. Talk to your players and see if they know anybody they can give you a clue on." We didn't have the money to talk to any of these recruits on the phone, so we had to write them letters.

Joe was doing the linemen, and I was doing the backs. I called my group of guys together and told them we were looking for a center and a quarterback. Two of our freshman kids had played in the B League in Pittsburgh, and they said, "There's a kid at Saint Justin's, his name's Unitas, John Unitas, and he has the guts of a burglar and he can really throw that football." That's the first time anyone in Louisville, Kentucky, had heard of John Unitas.

At Christmastime I was going back to my home in Sharon, Pennsylvania, and Coach Camp asked me to stop off in Pittsburgh and take a look at this Unitas kid. I had written some letters off to people in that area, including some other coaches, and one of those guys told me he had never even heard of Unitas. Another guy said, "Yeah, that kid's good. I've seen him play."

When we got to the Unitas house, John wasn't there. So we went over to the gym, where he was working out. With these two guys in tow, I went back to the Unitas house and met his mother, Helen, a remarkable woman. We sat down and I talked with her for about an hour and a half, and before I left I promised her two things—something that a young coach probably should not promise—that he would go to Mass every Sunday and that he would graduate.

I knew that Indiana University was after him, and I think he really wanted to go to Pittsburgh, but he couldn't make the grades. He couldn't pass the entrance exam. In the meantime, I paid the visit and kept writing to him.

In 1951 I got a letter from Helen Unitas saying John wanted to come to Louisville. It wasn't a recruiting coup for us. We got him because nobody else wanted him. He was five-ten, in my opinion, and weighed about 135 pounds. Joe Trabue built John up, and by the time he left school he weighed 190.

We had never seen him play, not in person, not on film. When Coach Camp first saw John, he turned to us and said, "You've really got a project to work on this time."

Not only was Unitas undersized by major-college standards, even those in 1951, he also was not a brilliant student. **SHIRLEY GREEN,** his sister:

A lot of the Ivy League schools came to our house to meet John, but he didn't have the grades. In fact, they were a deterrent to his getting into a lot of schools. He tried hard, but school was never really high enough on his list of priorities.

Joe Chilleo, another of John's high school classmates and a Pittsburgh neighbor in Mount Washington, says that even though he was playing in near-anonymity, Unitas harbored high aspirations:

You can look back now and see that John wanted something and was very, very driven to achieve it. But no one talked about it or thought about it at the time. Pro football was just too far from our world.[5]

2

~~~~~~~~

BLUEGRASS AND
SANDLOTS

At the time John Unitas left high school for college in 1951, the world of college football was already awash in great traditions and programs steeped in success. East of Pittsburgh there was West Point, where the Army Cadets of Earl "Red" Blaik still ruled and where an unknown assistant by the name of Vince Lombardi was starting to make a name for himself.

Some 350 miles west of Pittsburgh was the hamlet of South Bend, Indiana, where the Notre Dame Fighting Irish, most recently under Frank Leahy, were continuing on a path of dominance that had begun decades earlier under Knute Rockne.

Farther west and a bit to the south was the newest national powerhouse, the Oklahoma Sooners, who under Bud Wilkinson were embarking on a forty-seven-game winning streak that today remains a major-college football record. Forty-seven—that number would later become closely identified with John Unitas's Hall of Fame pro career.

Then there was Paul "Bear" Bryant, an up-and-coming coach at the University of Kentucky who within a decade would become a genuine coaching legend at the University of Alabama.

This was the era into which Unitas stepped, although it wasn't the world of which he would come a part. For the most part, the big schools ignored Unitas. Nothing against him, really; they just hadn't heard of him. Coming out of a Catholic high school, Unitas got the obligatory look-see at Notre Dame, but even that wasn't with any real expectations on either side. Some say it was Unitas's scrawny physique that turned off the Irish; others suggested it might have been his grades.

Whatever the reason(s), Unitas would soon be headed south to the University of Louisville, a midlevel program that was about to have the financial rug pulled out from beneath it. Anonymity would continue to be a Unitas companion.

***

JOE TRABUE, *also a former Louisville player, was a graduate-assistant coach there when Unitas arrived in 1951:*

The reason John Unitas hadn't made a big name for himself by the time he got to Louisville was that he came from a small high school, and John must have weighed maybe 150 or 160 pounds on his six-foot-two frame. He was as thin as a rail.

Early in the fifties, the only people that were interested in doing the things necessary to gain weight, other than just eating a lot, were the guys who had come back from the military. In the military, those guys had been exposed to a lot of people who liked weight training.

I was freshman line coach at the time, and I was teaching a weight-training class. We had an informal weight-training program with some of our athletes in the off-season. There was a group of freshmen who got together, and John was one of those who came by to work out with the weights. We were certainly hoping that he would get stronger and bigger, although he already had a tremendous arm. He could throw the ball on a rope about as deep as you wanted him to.

To determine what his true potential was, I could see several things in John. Number one, John was coachable. That's important. Number two, John had good peripheral vision, could recognize patterns, and could see the field developing before him. A quarterback couldn't afford to have tunnel vision. The third thing was his desire, which was a great asset for him.

By the time John graduated, he had played against enough good teams, like Tennessee and Florida State, for anyone who watched him to know that he was an outstanding player with good pro potential. He had the whole package, including being hard-nosed.

CLARK WOOD, *one of head coach Frank Camp's assistants at Louisville, gives some background on the football program up to 1951, setting the stage for John Unitas's arrival there:*

We had only three coaches in those days, like most other college football programs. We also taught physical education, and I was head track coach most of the time that I was there.

We played in what was called the Ohio Valley Conference, made up mostly of teams from Kentucky. We were classified as a small-college football program, and we never had more than about thirty-five or forty players on the team. We played schools like Xavier and Dayton. We played Cincinnati a couple of times, as well as some of the schools that now make up the Mid-American Conference.

Coach Camp came here in 1946, when they reinstituted the football program after World War II. I came here in 1947. By the late forties and 1950, we were playing some other schools as well, and the highlight of that time came when we tied Miami (Florida), 13–13, in 1950, and they went on to play in the New Year's Day Orange Bowl game that year.

In 1951 we started out not being able to score, even though we thought we had a pretty good football team. That's why, eventually, we put in Johnny Unitas to play as a freshman. We needed the leadership, and we needed the ability to throw the football. It was a complete turnaround when we put John in there, and we beat four good football teams in a row.

Louisville head football coach **FRANK CAMP** *had actually met Unitas the year before, when Unitas accompanied his high school coach at Camp's request to the 1950 Miami-Pittsburgh game to scout the Hurricanes for a game later that year. In a 1980 interview, long after he had ended his coaching career with a 118–95–2 overall mark at Louisville, Camp (who was succeeded as U of L coach by future ESPN analyst Lee Corso) explained how he gave Unitas a football scholarship, pretty much sight unseen, only to find that he had his work cut out for him once he saw the skinny freshman on his own football field at Louisville:*

We did not see films. Most high schools did not have them. You had to take somebody's word. Most of the time the coaches knew a good football player—some coaches would push a player who wasn't that good, but you had to know your coaches. I would talk to those who had played against the player and ask what they thought.

John was six-foot-one. He had big hands and big feet, lean, a lot of potential. He weighed 145 pounds when he came here. He was probably the first quarterback ever put on weights. I had him on a punching bag and jumping rope. He picked up weight and was 185 pounds by his sophomore year.

He was tough. He wanted to play. He wanted to be a professional football player, and he didn't mind work. He listened to what you told him, which is a great asset. That summer he came down here and took a job with Brown and Williamson. He stayed here at the university in a dorm. I spent a couple of hours every day working with him, throwing the ball and on fundamentals. I figured he had to be a good boy to be willing to stay the summer here on campus with nobody around and nothing to do. He convinced me he wanted to play.[1]

FRANK GITSCHIER had also played quarterback under Camp and, as an assistant coach, had a front-row seat to Camp's tutelage of the young Unitas:

Coach Frank Camp made Johnny Unitas what he is. This was an offensive-minded coach, but he came up with some great defenses, too. He could spread fields; we had one-back sets. John told me one time that after he had gotten to the Colts, Weeb Ewbank said, "We're going to put this formation in; do you think you can handle it, John?" He said, "Coach, I ran that back in college."

That's how advanced we were. Coach Camp made a quarterback out of me, and he prepared Johnny Unitas for the bigs. Coach Camp deserves a lot of the credit, and John would say the same thing many times.

One time when I was coaching, Coach Camp and Blanton Collier, who had at one time coached against each other in high school, became very close friends. One time Blanton came down here, and all our coaches sat there for three and a half hours spellbound while these two guys went back and forth on the blackboard.

The whole discussion was based on Coach Camp's philosophy, which he used more with Unitas than he had with me because John was a better passer than me. The basic fundamentals that came out of that conversation were screen, pass, trap, draw. You run those four things, and you coordinate them, and you run your offense. When they think you're going to pass, you run the draw; and when they think you're going to run the draw, you run the screen.

Coach changed a lot of things to fit what John could do.

Louisville assistant coach **JOE TRABUE**:

I don't know if it changed Coach Camp's offensive philosophy that much; only, we now had a great passer. We still ran our regular offense with sweeps and traps, but we cut back on the pitchouts. And there's no question that we threw the ball more when we had Unitas in there.

It was very effective passing. We threw the ball deep, we did screens to keep the pressure off the quarterback, and we also did regular pass patterns. The problem we sometimes ran into was pass blocking; sometimes John didn't have enough time back there to get off a good throw.

Unitas had to wait his turn at Louisville, despite an impressive showing during preseason drills. The Cardinals opened with a victory at Wayne State but then lost consecutive games to Boston University, Cincinnati, and Xavier. Down 19–0 to Saint Bonaventure, Camp had finally had enough—and in came John Unitas. **FRANK GITSCHIER** *remembers:*

At that point, Coach Camp said, "We're not going anywhere with these kids. You get that Unitas kid ready to play," and I did. John threw three touchdown passes to put us ahead, 21–19. Saint Bonny then kicked a field goal and missed, but somehow the clock didn't run out, so they kicked again and made it, and beat us, 22–21.

From that time on, John started. He threw five touchdown passes against Houston, in a 35–28 victory, including a ninety-two–yarder that is still in the school's record book. We ended the season 5–4, and that was the only decent team at Louisville on which John played, and that's because we still had remnants of the good guys we had had in 1948, 1949, and 1950.

By the way, that Saint Bonaventure team that beat us had a quarterback by the name of Ted Marchibroda, who subsequently went into the military service. Later, John was drafted in the ninth round by the Pittsburgh Steelers, and they now had three quarterbacks—John was the third one. When Marchibroda came out of the service, they gave John ten dollars and sent him home. Small world, huh?

You know what John did with the ten dollars? Instead of spending it on a bus to take home, he hitchhiked home because his wife was pregnant and they needed the ten dollars.

GITSCHIER continues:

John was the greatest blue-collar guy ever to play football. He came every day to get it done, and that was his job. That's what he said.

Coach Camp had taken one look at him and said, "Your boy don't look too good." Well, we took care of that. We worked with him real hard. One of his greatest attributes, and he had a lot of them, was that you had to tell him something only once.

I went right to John after practice and started working with him on some fundamentals, such as how far to bring the ball up to pass it and stepping toward the target. One thing John could do was throw that ball. Since then we have had guys at Louisville like Dave Ragone, Chris Redman, and Browning Nagle, and they all could hum it, but not like John. That's what made John so famous—that arm of his. And he had great timing, too.

The players he played with . . . it didn't make any difference to him. He got beat up and just figured that was a part of playing football, and that's just the way it is.

John was just one of those guys *made* to be a quarterback. No doubt about it.

We had a quarterback in here named Jerry Nassano. You could look at him and say, "Here's a kid who has had some coaching," and then you look at Unitas and you wonder what's up. Nassano was a good kid and so much better prepared fundamentally. But once John came around, Jerry saw the writing on the wall, and he ended up playing at Western Kentucky. I think he even played against Unitas one year.

CLARK WOOD was an assistant coach at the University of Louisville when Unitas came to town:

Once he got here and got in practice, you knew when you saw him throw the ball that there was something different about him. I'm not sure even we knew exactly what it was, only that we figured that, somehow, this was a guy that we needed. He could throw the tight spiral and the long ball. That started giving Coach Camp some ideas.

He was a skinny little thing when he came to us, but he developed very quickly. All the time he played with us, he looked great, even when we had a poor team. We would have passed the ball more with him had we had the receivers to do it with, but instead we had to run the ball more than we would have liked. Our favorite running series was the outside belly series. John could fake the off-tackle play and then throw from there. We couldn't have done anything by just dropping back and throwing.

FRANK GITSCHIER recalls how Unitas almost walked out on Frank Camp after Camp had punished him for drinking water after practice:

We had three-hour practices, and the players weren't allowed to drink any water, but John thought it was okay because practice was over. Camp yelled out, "Unitas, that's five laps around the field!" Boy, John was mad. I knew what was about to happen. He was going to go back to Williams Street. I ran with him and said, "John, this is what makes you tough." He finally calmed down.[2]

GITSCHIER:

Coach Camp fell in love with him. And what wasn't there to love? John was the first of those lunch-pail quarterbacks to come out of western Pennsylvania. Later on came Jim Kelly and Dan Marino and Joe Namath and Joe Montana. They were all the same: guys who didn't have anything, guys who knew that it was back to the steel mills or coal mines if they didn't get the job done.[3]

One of Unitas's Louisville teammates was **HAL BETHEA,** *who had arrived there in 1949 and was two years ahead of John:*

I was a 215–pound tackle. To me, he looked like a kid, really young. He was long and lanky, and he was sort of tow-headed. Actually, he looked more country than he did as somebody who just came from Pittsburgh.

John didn't play in the early games of his freshman year. But Coach Frank Camp had been working on a passing attack. There was no such thing as a pro set in those days, but Coach Camp invented something like a pro set, I'm sure in some part because of what he saw emerging in Johnny.

In practice one day after Coach Camp had made Johnny the starter, we were practicing some pass blocking. One of our guys on the offensive line wasn't doing his job in blocking this big ol' guy we had on defense by the name of (Bob) Bender, and Bender was hitting Unitas pretty regularly. Finally, one of the coaches asked the whole team if there was anybody present who could block Bender, and, stupid me, I said, "Yes, I can." I hadn't played first string yet, and now I was about to get my chance.

Well, I got up there and was able to block Bender, who weighed about 250. It was a matter of sacrificing myself to the cause. After that, I made the first team because of pass blocking, and I played with Johnny the rest of the year and the following season.

At Louisville, Unitas wasn't surrounded by a lot of talent, but he made a lot of friends. That's Johnny in back, number 18. Included in the photo are brothers Reggie (63) and Hal (70) Bethea, as well as Lavelle Smith (54).

Johnny was amazing. We had what we called a split offense, with only one running back, Jim Williams. That's what made it so hard to pass block, having only one back back there to help out. We had one wideout on one side and another wideout on the other side, with two other backs split out, and they were all pass receivers. So we had four receivers going out for passes on practically every play. It looked like a pro set, except the pro set has two backs in the backfield.

I remember one game we had against Washington and Lee in 1951. I missed a block on one play, and in the huddle before the next play, Unitas looked straight at me and said, "Bethea, you've got to block this guy this time," and then he gave us the play. I had to pull out on the play, in which John was going to run toward the sideline. I made the block on that guy on the play, and Unitas was able to run it in for the touchdown.

Even as a freshman and sophomore, he was one of those guys who could really lead a team. He was in control, and it was almost like he could coach you in the huddle. Not too many young guys could do that, but even then he was a field general. He had so much confidence in himself—a lot of it rubbed off on the rest of us. I still have the picture showing me making the block on that touchdown run of Johnny's, and it has been a constant reminder to me over the years of what kind of field general Johnny was.

BETHEA:

John wasn't a real standout when he got here, not one of those guys who came here with the idea that he would start the first game. I don't think the coaches realized that this was a guy, a young recruit, who could go right out there and take over the team. He had been a good quarterback in high school, but his coming to Louisville didn't exactly wow a lot of folks. If he had been that highly regarded, I'm sure the coaches would already have told us that, because that's the way they were.

Coach Camp had a great football mind. He wasn't a Knute Rockne, I guess, but he had a great head for football. He had a futuristic look at football and was able to see what would work down the road as opposed to just the here and now. He knew from the beginning that Johnny had a great arm, but he didn't know that he was ready to start. But when he put Johnny into that Saint Bonaventure game, he knew what he had. A gutsy guy, who even on third or fourth down on his own thirty would call a darn pass play. And he'd complete it!

Johnny could easily throw the ball fifty yards, and he could throw it to the right place—not to the man—but right to where the receiver was supposed to be at that instant, just like they do in the pros now. That was Camp's idea, and that's how his ideas meshed so well with what he had in Johnny as his quarterback and his ability to throw.

———

There certainly was no mistaking the University of Louisville for one of the major college football powers of the day. First of all, the school itself wasn't structured to accommodate big-time football. It didn't have the money, nor did it have football as a high priority.
CLARK WOOD:

Louisville was a small city school and didn't get any aid from anything other than student tuition. Most of the players we recruited were local, mostly from Kentucky. We didn't have enough money to recruit anywhere else. It's not that the university wouldn't give it to us—they didn't have it to give to us. The sport wasn't paying for itself.

———

WALTER FIGHTMASTER *was a couple of years older than Unitas and had come out for football, but he gave up wearing the pads to help sort them out as a student manager in the athletic department. He helps to paint the picture of Louisville football circa 1950:*

In the late forties we had been quite competitive with other schools in the Ohio Valley Conference but not nationally. We played on a football field that was part of the same facility used by the Louisville Colonels; what we used as dormitories was what was left over from the navy's V-12 program; and the gym we had was, by even those days' standards, antiquated. I guess it's fair to say we were in tough times.

There was more support for basketball than there was for football, even then, because this has always been a basketball state first. Football would get its shot in the arm by John Unitas coming on board, although what he sparked did not occur until after he left here and became much better known.

FIGHTMASTER, on Unitas:

One of my first impressions from watching him when he first got here was that he had a tremendous arm. The ends had a difficult time catching the ball because he threw so hard. There was some griping from guys, mainly related to the fact that he was difficult to catch. But he wasn't the first-string quarterback that first year.

Not long after Unitas arrived at Louisville, school officials decided to de-emphasize the football program. Dr. Philip G. Davidson had become school president in 1951, and he quickly made it clear he was no football fan. In January 1952, at Davidson's prodding, the board of trustees voted to significantly reduce and limit its fiscal responsibility for football and other inter-collegiate sports. Under the new policy, financial aid to athletes would come only in the form of paid tuition, and athletes were to receive no preference in the awarding of scholarships. Additionally, higher academic standards eliminated about twenty football players from the team, leaving a program that for the next three years of Unitas's stay there would be severely outmanned and undersized on the football field. **CLARK WOOD** remembers:

A lot of people on that team left school, and most of them came off the defense. There had been this big hullabaloo about our spending too much money on football, and the university was too poor a school. So after John's first year at Louisville, we didn't bring in another player on scholarship until 1954. John had offers from other schools to transfer out, but he stayed here out of loyalty, even though he knew it would be detrimental to him in terms of individual publicity and setting him up for a shot at pro football.

At the same time, the schedule, which was already in place, had been upgraded to where we were now playing teams like Tennessee and Florida State. We were committed to playing those games, and we managed to beat Florida State in 1952 (during a 3–5 season). We had a good offense but no defense. And we were even worse in 1953 (1–7). Then, in 1954, the school renewed the scholarships for football. We won only three games that year, but almost everybody who was playing that year was a freshman.

JOE TRABUE:

There was a sense that anything being spent for the athletic program was taking away from academics. You would think they were trying to kill football. There was a sense of loss and disappointment.

Eventually, two things happened. Coach Camp went before the faculty senate and he said, "Let's get rid of football, if this is what you want to do. Otherwise, stop this bickering about whether or not we're going to have a football program next year." That got things moving in the right direction. Coach Camp started meeting with the business people in the community, and they started getting behind the team.

*Louisville native **FRANK OTTE** was one of the players who came aboard during the lean years, in 1953. He had a chance to play for Bear Bryant at Kentucky but changed his mind to stay close to home. So he turned his back on the Bear and got a shot at playing along-side with Unitas instead. Otte provides more insight about what Louisville was like in the fifties:*

Louisville was what you would call a streetcar college. A lot of people lived off campus, as I did a lot of the time. Most people there didn't know the football players even when they saw them around, except perhaps for some of the professors.

It wasn't a high-profile thing to be a football player. The football player didn't always get the girl—he was like any other guy on campus trying to get by. Football didn't have much to do with what went on during everyday life as a student.

In those days we didn't have mouthpieces. We didn't even have a bar over the facemask yet. You had a lot of guys with broken noses and missing teeth in those days.

I belonged to a fraternity—Delta Epsilon—and a lot of football players didn't belong to fraternities then. We had a couple of football players who belonged to my fraternity, but it was a good social experience. I would hang out with football players and I'd also hang out with frat brothers. It was a good, rounded education for me.

*
HAL BETHEA recalls how a big crowd at a University of Louisville football game would be fifteen thousand, although attendance usually was about half that:*

Even back then, Louisville was a basketball school, much like it is still today. But the football program has done quite well in recent years, closing the gap somewhat with basket-ball in terms of popularity and success.

Some people in and around Louisville can actually dream now of having at least a shot at a national champi-onship in football, as well as in basketball again, and I have to think that that all somehow goes back to what Johnny Unitas did for the school about fifty years ago.

We were playing some pretty good schools in the late forties and early fifties, and were able to hold our own against a lot of them, in large part because of Coach Camp, too. He was the kind of person who would give any guy a chance. He thought of you as more than just a ballplayer. He wanted to help you, too. He was the kind of guy who might come to your room and say something like, "Bethea, I noticed that you didn't have a topcoat when we got on the plane the other day. You take this note down to this clothing store in downtown Louisville and get yourself a topcoat."

One thing about Johnny that I remember is that every Sunday morning, Johnny would get up early, get dressed, and go to Catholic Mass. I was raised a Baptist in Birming-ham and didn't know many Catholics, but I do know that he was one of the few guys on the team going to church every Sunday. I honor Johnny for doing that; I'm sure he was doing what his mama had taught him to do. I can't say for certain how early he was getting up to go, but I do know that we had to have our breakfast eaten no later than nine o'clock, and I know he wouldn't eat until after he had been to Mass.

The school restored its football scholarship program in 1954, and one of its first new, out-of-state recruits was **TOM ARMSTRONG,** *who had run track and played end on his high school football team in Dayton, Ohio. Armstrong:*

That summer after graduating from high school, I had a nice visit with the coaches down there in Louisville, and when the fall came and it was time to get ready for practice, I came back down and interviewed with the coaches. Then they took me over to see this fellow sitting on some steps, and they said, "If you have any problems or any questions and don't feel like you can come to the coaching staff with them, we want you to see this fellow." That was my introduction to John Unitas.

I didn't know who he was, although he was somewhat famous there, getting ready to enter his senior year as a well-established local hero. I got to know John quite well in the short time we were at Louisville together, with our rooming across from each other. We spent quite a bit of time together. Even though I was only a freshman, I roomed with a guy who was a junior and who had been in the service for four years before that, so I grew up pretty quickly being around those guys.

Having John as our quarterback was like having a coach in the huddle. He was so knowledgeable about everything going on in a game as well as what everybody else was supposed to be doing at their respective positions. He was just a take-control guy, and when he said something, you listened. He was very forceful in that way.

There were many times where we went on the road for games and the public-address announcers would have trouble pronouncing his name, like "YOU-nuh-tiss." He took it in stride. He was just a hard-nosed ballplayer, and he played defense as well as offense. Halfway through that season (1954), he broke his ankle. Not totally, but bad enough to lay up most people. John just taped it up and played.

He might have been one of the most unlikely looking athletes, but he sure could play and he was tough. He played defensive back as well. I remember one game against Florida

State when they were romping us. They threw a ball toward the sideline, and John ran over there, jumped up, and grabbed the ball out of bounds but while still in the air threw the ball back to one of our other guys in-bounds, like a lateral. You see plays like that in basketball quite a bit, but I had never seen a play like that in football, not before or since. It was one of those kinds of instinctive things that he did that just made you say, "Wow."

ARMSTRONG, *with more on Unitas:*

I would see him fire the ball so hard in practice that he would knock guys' helmets off sometimes. It was like a rocket, and their helmet would go flying off. That was one more reason to pay attention, to do your job.

He had big hands and a big upper body, which you wouldn't suspect by looking at the rest of his body. His hands were so big that he could grip the ball at the laces and still touch the tip of the ball with his index finger.

John was the same in practice as he was in a game: serious. He never kidded around. You did your job. He was as respected as any of the coaches were, if not more. When he wasn't on the field, he was one of the guys, sometimes kidding around with the rest of us. He was just fun to be with.

REGGIE BETHEA, *Hal Bethea's younger brother, also went to the University of Louisville and was in the same class as Unitas:*

Johnny had a marvelous arm. We knew he was a professional from the time he first walked on the field. He was a commander. The rest of us were just players—this guy had more than that. He had a maturity, moxie, a certain power about him. But once he took his uniform off, he became something less than what we were—a totally unassuming guy who tended to stay in the background. How he turned it on and off like that, I don't know.

REGGIE BETHEA *oftentimes found himself paying more attention to what Unitas happened to be doing than tending to what he himself should be doing:*

I used to see him stand on the fifty-yard line with a bunch of footballs and a basket hanging off the crossbar of the goalposts at the end of the field, and he was able to put most of those balls in the basket with his throws. His accuracy was amazing.

REGGIE BETHEA *offers some additional insight into college life at Louisville:*

All of the old buildings that I knew from my days at Louisville are now gone. The campus was beginning to grow, but the university was split up. Most of us, like Johnny and me, were on the Arts and Sciences campus, while the medical school was across town. They have since bought much of the land in between, and the campus is now, more or less, combined.

Coach Frank Camp was a real football coach, although he never worried about winning. I never heard him get upset when he knew we were going to lose. I never saw him look at us and say, "We have to win this game." Did he want to win? Of course he did, but he didn't make a big deal out of it.

One of my favorite stories in life involved Coach Camp. I had flunked my entrance exam at Louisville, after having been captain of my high school football team and an all-stater. My mother wanted me to go to school, but I did not want to go. I was only there because my mom wanted me to be there. I wanted to go into the navy instead, and I was elated when I flunked my entrance exam.

Coach Camp asked me what had happened with my test, and I told him that I had blown it. He said, "I'm sorry," and I said, "Well, I'm not."

"Why?"

"So I can now go back to Birmingham."

"What's back there? Now that you're out of high school, what are you going to do back there?"

This was stuff I didn't want to hear. He then said, "I got a call from Corrine—is that your mother?"

"Yes, sir."

"Did you call her?"

"Yes, sir."

"Why did you call her?"

"Because she's going to be upset."

"She was crying when I talked to her. I want you to shut up with this business about not wanting to be here, because if you have to go back, I want you to know that your mother's heart is going to be broken."

"Yes, sir."

"You look at me, and don't smile when you talk to me."

"Yes, sir."

"Tell you what, do you want to be at the University of Louisville?"

"No, sir."

"What do you want to do?" and we went all the way through that argument again.

"Reggie, your mother wants you to go to school. If I can work it out that you can go to school, will you go?"

"Yes, sir."

"Well, I thought you said you didn't want to go."

"I do want to go, coach."

"By the way, I don't want you, either, but Corrine wants you here. She's a wonderful woman. But I don't like your attitude."

"Coach, I don't like yours."

"Tell you what, if I keep you here, would you stay?"

"Coach, I will, and I'll try to be your best player and not make another sound about not wanting to be here."

"Okay."

And they worked it out for me to go to school there, although I wouldn't be able to go home during the summer for two years so I could do some makeup work.

When I first got there, I didn't like Coach Camp's mannerisms, but he was truthful. There are very few urban legends about Coach Camp because he didn't have all the (won-lost) stats that some other coaches did, but he was a coach genuinely concerned with how we would turn out.

That place looked like a Greyhound bus station. He would get in fifty players and get rid of thirty or forty of them that couldn't measure up.

Coach Camp and Johnny got along beautifully. We didn't win many games, so he didn't get a lot of notice in terms of wins and losses, but he was known as a terrific football player. You knew he wanted to play pro football, and he could have helped himself a lot in that regard by transferring to another program, but he didn't. His loyalty was to Louisville and Coach Camp, even though he had no chance of making All-American there.

RAY FARMER was a year behind Unitas at Louisville:

We called him "Mr. Sparkplug." He was the type of person who wanted everything done right, and he was a team leader.

He was the sparkplug of the team. Sportswriters called him "Mr. Football."

Johnny was a quiet person. He wore blue jeans just like all the rest of us guys who were poor. Later on in life, when I would see him, he almost always had nice clothes on, along with a sport coat. That was the only change in him—his personality never changed. When we had been back at college, we were all wearing hightop shoes at that time, you know. The difference with Johnny is that he continued wearing them after everyone else had gone to the lowcuts.

FARMER played end on both sides of the ball, but mostly on defense. He recalls practicing with Unitas:

We practiced right on campus on a makeshift field, right outside the old wooden barracks we lived in as dorms. Coach Camp had hard practices. Johnny was always intense, putting out 100 percent, and he didn't mind getting on you if you did something wrong, even in practice. If he put a ball in your hands, he expected you to catch it. He could throw bullets, although he could also drop it in there nice and softly, and long passes. He had great touch, and he was very accurate.

Football was a business to John. He was serious about it and always confident about what he could do. Some people might have even thought of him as conceited, but you never heard Johnny brag on himself. He was not an outgoing person. And he was always a team player.

MICHAEL MCDONALD, now a retired judge still living in Louisville, was another homegrown product who went to the University of Louisville starting in 1954. He

was a freshman when Unitas was a senior, yet that age
gap didn't keep the two from becoming pals:

John was always a religious person; there was nothing dirty about him. Always a gentleman. But he was a tough football player, real tough.

He was hidden at Louisville because the program, for all practical purposes, had ceased. He didn't have any seasoned players to go with him. With the personnel they had originally brought in, they would have beaten Tennessee (in 1953, when they lost, 59–6), and the following year they would have been a power team, probably top twenty-five. Instead, John got lost because he didn't have any stats and his team wasn't playing in any bowl games.

FRANK OTTE *further explains why he changed his*
mind about going to Kentucky and shares what he
discovered about what kind of player John Unitas was:

I played high school ball at Saint Xavier's High School here in Louisville—I played center and linebacker—and actually had a scholarship to go to the University of Kentucky. Bear Bryant was up there then, and I think everybody and his brother was going to Kentucky. In fact, the governor came down and recruited a couple of players from Louisville, but he never came to see me, and that kind of hurt my feelings a little bit. So I figured I would just go to the University of Louisville.

I had a brother-in-law who played ball at Kentucky, and I asked him how many of their guys were graduating. He told me about five or six would graduate each year, and I knew they were starting out with about 150 each year, so I knew the graduation rate was pretty poor. I figured maybe it was better for me to stay home and do my thing at the University of Louisville.

The first thing I remember about Unitas is how he stayed out after practice and took snaps with me. He would stay out until dark, by which time everybody else would be in eating supper. We did this almost every day for two weeks before the start of the season, about thirty minutes to an hour at a time. We would start with the cadence count and then I would snap him the ball, just to give him the feel. The exchange between the center and the quarterback is pretty important, and he knew that. We just kept working on it and got it down to a fine art. John was willing to stay out and work extra with anybody, anything to help the team along.

Luckily, I got to start some games my freshman year at center. But we didn't have a very good year—I think we won one game all season (19–14 over Murray State to open the season, followed by seven consecutive losses). Our ranks were thin, and we had some older guys coming back from the Korean War; you had a funny combination of really young guys and other guys, war veterans, a lot older.

OTTE remembers the Cardinals' 59–6 loss in 1953 to Tennessee at Knoxville:

In those days we had to go both ways. I was playing line-backer, too, and when we played Tennessee down in Knoxville, they had that double-wing offense then, in which they would pull their guards and had two blockers leading the charge through the hole. I saw my end being taken out and my guard being taken in, and you could have driven a semi-truck through the hole that was created. They came running over me like I wasn't even there, and moments later I would be looking up from down on the ground and see

Unitas loved playing golf, was committed to supporting charities, and enjoyed being around his former Louisville teammates. Here he is hitting the trifecta. On the far right is Frank Otte, who was a Unitas teammate with the Cardinals for two seasons.

Johnny Unitas down the field making the tackle. He played safety and was actually a pretty good defensive player. He must have been pretty agile to get away from all those blockers to be able to make the tackle.

OTTE *says he has no regrets about choosing Louisville over Kentucky, even with two dismal seasons his first two years there:*

It was close to home, and it was a really good school. I was in it more for the scholarship and the education. My family wasn't very well off when I was growing up. I had four sisters and an aunt who lived with us, and I wasn't from a really athletic family. I was just glad to have an opportunity to play some sports, and football was the only sport I was any good at. You couldn't beat the deal, having a football scholarship to Louisville. Even in losing, we played the best we could and enjoyed it. Of course, at the time, I didn't know that Johnny Unitas would go on to bigger and better things.

It's funny: I hadn't heard much about him until I got there. In fact, I didn't know anything about many of the Louisville players, even though I had gone to high school there.

*The first thing that struck **OTTE** about Unitas when he first saw the young quarterback was a physical appearance that belied his athletic prowess:*

John was a pretty skinny guy, but he was really athletic. I remember seeing him in the gym hitting the punching bag, the small one at eye level, and he could really get that thing going. He had great hand-eye coordination.

Hitting the punching bag wasn't a typical workout for football players, but John wasn't your typical football player. At the time I was watching him, I was thinking about how I would hate to get into a fight with him. He could've punched you four times before you knew what hit you.

John had a strong upper body, and he must have been strong all the way through to take those blows like he did all those years in the NFL. He was a guy determined to do what he wanted to do, and he did it. You don't see that in a lot of guys, those who would follow through.

John didn't have anywhere near the level of support in college that he would have had playing at Notre Dame or under Bear Bryant at Kentucky. It's fun to speculate and wonder what would have happened if John had been taken at Notre Dame—that might have changed how things worked out for Paul Hornung, even though Hornung was a year or two younger. You just never know.

***

TOM ARMSTRONG lived across the hall from Unitas
in a dorm:

It was fun. We lived football and sports, and we managed to work in some school when we could.

We lived in old barracks buildings that had been converted into dorms. They were doing a lot of renovation in those days, digging a lot of stuff up. There were times that John and I would drag a mattress out onto the lawn and sit in the sun to get away from all the mess. There wasn't much else for us to do.

Some of us guys might wrestle around some or go into town to catch a movie, but most of the guys were pretty well broke, and there wasn't much you could do without some cash in pocket. I did have one buddy who was on the G.I. bill, and after he got his monthly check I would help him spend that.

Then again, there were a lot of things given to us that were free, such as going to the movies or going downtown to a restaurant. We got a lot of perks that way, as well as what they called laundry money, and the more sports you played the more laundry money you got. Of course, it was nothing that you got paid in the form of a check.

***

Unitas's college pal **MICHAEL MCDONALD** describes
Louisville as a "streetcar school":

It closed up, literally, at noon Friday and didn't open back up until Monday morning. There were no campus activities over the weekend, except for the games.

You gotta realize, this was almost the Dark Ages, still. In football, you had to play both ways and didn't have face-masks. I can remember one time I broke my nose in the Tennessee game, and the next week they put me in one of those cages for your head. I think it was Chattanooga we played the next week, and they had a bunch of renegades who had been kicked out at Alabama for panty raids.

There I was with this big cage on me, and it didn't take those guys two minutes to figure out I had something wrong up there. Their hands were going up into my helmet doing all kinds of stuff to me. When I finally got to the sideline, I said, "Get this thing off of me; they're killing me!"

Plus, we were decimated size-wise in terms of number of personnel. We had a rule then that when you went out, you couldn't return to play in that quarter. Our opponents would run whole teams in and out, using a six-minute team, a four-minute team, and a two-minute team, or something like that. Us? We would have to stay out there the whole time.

We could hang with these people, but we would wear down. John could flat-out control a game, but we would run out of steam, and the roof would fall in on us in the third quarter. We might be losing, but not by much, and then the air would go out of us. Except for Johnny—he ended up making more tackles than anyone else on the team, and he was supposed to be camouflaged back there. He would have been better off playing linebacker.

Put him on the other side of the ball, though, and Unitas would take the fight to you. **McDonald:**

John was bright, knew the game so well, knew tendencies, and he could quickly pick up what the other side was doing. He was great at figuring out where he had to throw to. It was amazing. He would check off a lot at the line. He knew what he was doing. He was just overwhelmed by the caliber of teams we had to go up against.

Among the other men whose names have long been closely associated with Unitas's are Raymond Berry and Lenny Moore, teammates of his with the Baltimore Colts. Another Colts teammate often linked with Unitas was **LENNY LYLES**, *who had also gone to Louisville, three years behind Unitas. Lyles:*

John was a senior when I got to Louisville. I went there as the school's first black scholarship athlete. I had gone to Central High School, a segregated school in Louisville.

I was a little concerned and apprehensive because I had been in a black environment all of my life. I had to pioneer a forest that I didn't know much about.

On the weekends, the school cafeteria wasn't open, so I told John and Jack Meade (also a teammate) that I was going out to my mom's place and they were welcome to join me for dinner. She didn't have a very big place, just a little flat out in the city. John didn't hesitate—he was ready to go. It was only a couple miles away and we could have walked if we had wanted to, but somebody always had a raggedy car to get us over there. We just jumped in and cruised over there.

So we went to my mom's, and she fixed us some greens, beets, potatoes, and stuff like that—a classic Southern, home-cooked meal. And I was able to get to know John pretty well, even after we both go to the Colts. I joined him there after being drafted number one by the Colts. When I got there, John would help me out with things and always ask about my mom. He never forgot those weekend meals.

LYLES was a prized recruit for Frank Camp and Louisville. He was strong with world-class speed, although with Unitas as a field general, he was just another cog in the machine:

John stacked up well against any other player in football, not just quarterbacks. There were guys who didn't tackle or block, but John had no qualms about the contact aspect of football. We had something called the Hamburger Drill, and it didn't matter who you were, you had to get into the middle of it. In the Hamburger Drill, one player was handed the ball to run straight ahead, and the guy on defense had to stand in there and tackle the ball carrier straight-on.

John could hit, and, boy, could he tackle. He could also throw with either arm. He was a *football* player, in all respects. No question about it.

MICHAEL McDONALD:

John didn't have much meat on his bones, but he was rawboned. When we had tackling practice, we were expected to really go after one another. I hated it when I had to go up against him, because it was like trying to tackle a steel pole. It hurt. He could really hurt you, and he hit hard. He really went after it.

McDONALD had something in common with his Louisville teammate Frank Otte: He, too, had originally

planned to go to Kentucky to play football for Bear
Bryant. McDonald provides some background, including
playing with a couple of guys who would become well-
known in their own right:

I went to Flaget High School in Louisville, a Catholic boys
high school. I played four years on the varsity, during which
time we won two state championships. Paul Hornung and
Howard Schnellenberger were two of the players who were
there at the time.

At first I got talked into going to the University of
Kentucky. Went out in 1953. It just didn't work out. I left
after two weeks, in part because my mother was home pretty
much by herself—my dad was a railroader traveling during
much of the week.

Louisville had had some real good teams and were building a strong program. Then they switched presidents, and Dr.
Phillip Davidson came in. He was anti-sports, anti-athletic,
anti-anything with a jock. Between the 1952 and 1953 seasons, when he came to the university, he booted out about
thirty junior and senior football players. He just said that their
grade-point average wasn't sufficient, and they were gone.

They had built up a major schedule, and now we didn't
have any upperclassmen playing, except for Unitas and a few
other guys. So who was left to play this big schedule other
than, basically, freshmen? I started right away, playing corner
on defense, and I played running back on offense. John played
defense, too, and I know they tried to "hide" him on defense,
so to speak, so he could get some rest, but we were so green
that he ended up having to make most of the tackles.

Away games could be an adventure even before the
team reached its destination. **McDonald:**

We traveled a lot. We would hire a training plane from Purdue University when they weren't using it. I distinctly remember flying into Knoxville and Tallahassee in that thing, and it about killed me. We got up so high that the fillings in my teeth would freeze. I was in agony for about two hours in those things. It had seats like today's planes, but it wasn't pressurized. We had guys getting sick. I don't remember John getting sick on those flights, though. He was just tough.

Part of being a tough guy meant keeping it inside when you were hurting, or even when you were winning. Even keel. That described Unitas, as **FRANK OTTE** *recalls:*

John was not a rah-rah type of guy. He was a man's man, and whatever he did he did it by leadership. I remember being on the road one time my first year there. John rounded up all the Catholic guys and told us, "It's time to go to church. There's an eight o'clock Mass, and we're going." This was the day after the game, and John would lead us off to church. Now that's leadership, getting a bunch of football players to go to church on a Sunday.

I also remember in the Florida State game, as a freshman being the first substitute in as a linebacker. Lee Corso was the quarterback for Florida State, and Burt Reynolds was playing for them, too, at the time. Now that was a combination. On the first play Corso hit me right in the belly with a pass; unfortunately, I dropped that one.

HAL BETHEA:

Johnny was probably the easiest-going serious person you ever saw. One of his good points that, even in the thick of it, like when the game was close or even if we were losing, he wasn't the kind of person who would get really upset. He might say something sharp to you on the field, but he did it in such a way that you wouldn't get angry with him. You knew he was right and that he was only doing what he felt was necessary to give us a better chance to win. He could correct you without ticking you off or making you react defensively. He was like this even as a freshman—he never lost it on the field.

Off the field, he was not what you would call one of those big-man-on-campus-type of guys. He didn't strut around campus or anything like that. He was not a braggart, nothing like that. He was a quiet kind of guy who didn't push himself on anybody. That attitude is probably what made him a good leader in the pros as well. On the other hand, I wouldn't think of him as a loner, either.

***

MICHAEL MCDONALD *was one of the few players who could lay claim to the distinction of having played both with a future Heisman Trophy winner (Paul Hornung in this case) and the future greatest NFL quarterback in history (Unitas):*

Paul Hornung was my high school quarterback and John Unitas my college quarterback, so I played with each name before they became famous. I was right there at the Creation, and I didn't even know it.

In a dichotomous way, the two complemented one another. We had a big team at Flaget; we would have been the second- or third-biggest team in the Southeastern Conference. Hornung was the ultimate college quarterback, but when he went pro he couldn't cut it as a quarterback. He had quick feet and could get outside and was a good ball handler, but the throwing had to be on the run—no dropback. So at Flaget and later at Notre Dame, he was the perfect quarterback because he could throw outside the tackles and keep the ball and run with it. Paul could drop back and throw if he had to, but it wouldn't fit our scheme at Flaget. He could throw, but he wasn't a deep thrower, and that explains why he ended up as a halfback for the Green Bay Packers.

On the other hand, Johnny would not have cut it in terms of being the consummate high school or college quarterback. Number one, below the waist he was awkward. He wasn't quick. But, boy, he could drop back on the five- or seven-step and get back there quickly. He couldn't throw outside the tackles, but he didn't have to. What he could do was hit you right in the mouth with a perfect pass from fifty-five yards away.

I knew when I came out of the backfield, with John at quarterback, I had to be twenty-five or thirty yards down the field by the time he was setting up to throw because that ball would just be flat-out coming at me. When we would do flag patterns, a sprint and go, you just ran and ran and then you would finally look up and there would be the ball coming, hitting you right in the hands. It was right there. Uncanny.

RAY FARMER *remembers Unitas as a cool cat on campus, as well:*

You might see Johnny just walking across campus, whistling, and he would stop and smile and speak to you.

When the game was on, though, so was Unitas.
FRANK OTTE:

John wouldn't really get on somebody bad, but he might ask some pretty pointed questions.

When Florida State came up here my sophomore year, it must have been about a hundred degrees. We kicked off—I was on the kickoff-coverage team—and the ball went out of bounds, so we had to come all the way back and kick off over again. Then I stayed on the field to play linebacker.

We finally got the ball, and that's when Unitas came back in. This was about the time we were phasing in playing only one side of the ball, so John was all rested up and ready to go. I was pretty much huffin' and puffin' by that time. He looked at me in the huddle and said, "What's wrong, Otte? Are you out of shape or something?" I said, "No, John, I've just been running a heckuva lot more than you have." He got a kick out of that.

MICHAEL MCDONALD:

You can imagine the level of ability he was having to put up with, with us as his teammates, with a lineup that was predominantly freshmen. Six of us were from the same high school team, and we were just kids. And we're playing Florida State and Tennessee.

Johnny was our daddy, our father figure. We had young kids, a tough schedule, and an anti-athletic administration. But we had Unitas. Other than having him, Louisville was a step down from Flaget.

The coaches were under pressure to save money. Each player was graded on film each week, and if we didn't get a passing grade, we didn't eat that week. We were taken off the food line. We had a bunch of kids who were poor. Some of the boys who hadn't made the grade that week would have to get up early and head to the grocery store, where every morning loaves of fresh bread had been put in the box, and they would steal a loaf of bread out of the breadbox. You had to get up around four-thirty or five o'clock to get there before the grocery store opened. When you're hungry, you've got to eat, especially at a time when you're going through so much physical exertion. It didn't make sense, but no one questioned it. That's just the way you did things.

It wasn't bad for me because I lived only about a mile away from home, and I could always go home to get something to eat. Johnny used to come home with me a lot to eat. My mom was a cook for the Bluegrass Cooperage Company. We got twenty-five dollars a month called laundry money, under NCAA rules. Well, you can just imagine that that money didn't go toward laundry. We got fifteen dollars a weekend because the university shut down at mealtime Friday and didn't open back up until breakfast on Monday.

I'd go home—I had a car. I had a steady stream of teammates coming home with me, and my mother didn't care because she was a cook and whatever was left over from the cafeteria, she would bring it home and feed it to us. That worked out pretty well, and so the guys could pocket their fifteen bucks and go do whatever.

JOE TRABUE remembers the four years Unitas was at Louisville as trying times—they kept trying to get things right, and sometimes they did.

In that four-year period in which John was at the university, he played some really tough ball clubs. One was the University of Tennessee, the year we played at Knoxville, particularly. We got beat really badly, but I remember their coach after the game saying, "It's obvious that there was one real man playing out there on that football field today," and he was talking about Johnny. Johnny had stayed in there under the most intense pressure you could imagine and delivered the football as best as he could.

That's how good John was—his team was getting slaughtered and he still showed how good he was as a football player.

As a coach, I had the opportunity to recommend players to the pros, and there were a couple teams interested—the Browns and the Steelers, and it helped that I had contacts there. But there was no way I could really convince them of the potential that Johnny had to play pro football. They just couldn't believe that this individual was that good. Their thinking was, *You're a small school and he may be an outstanding player in your eyes, but you're talking about playing with the big boys here.*

We could see and understand all that he could do, to include the so-called "small" things like footwork and field vision, but how do you put all that into words to pro scouts who had never seen him play? How do you get them to believe you, that it's not just a bunch of hype with a coach's looking out for one of his players with no sense of objectivity?

I wrote letters. That's how I contacted them. Evidently, I wasn't a very good writer because I didn't really sell them on Johnny.

Of course, there was more to going to school than just football. **MICHAEL MCDONALD** *recalls taking some courses with Unitas, which often could be an adventure as well:*

I remember one psychology class we took together because we had a professor by the name of Birdwhistle. That's the kind of name you don't easily forget.

I once thought Johnny was going to hammer Birdwhistle

after he made some remarks against Catholics, something about how the transubstantiation of the Mass involved a primitive cannibalistic instinct in man. Johnny didn't take it well, and he got up in the professor's face, right during class. John said, "I take offense to what you're saying."

Birdwhistle backed off and tried to sugarcoat some of it, but Johnny was still pretty upset. He calmed down after a while.

There was another class, a humanities class, where we, literally, had to hide the fact that we were athletes. There was a feeling that if the professor knew that you were a scholarship athlete, you weren't going to pass, or at least you weren't going to get a very good grade.

That perception permeated much of the campus, in fact. So we did not make it known under any method that we were athletes. We certainly avoided going into that classroom doing any macho stuff. I remember that Johnny was riding a B in that humanities class, and he thought he did real well on his final—I did, too—and we ended up with Cs or Ds, I'm not sure which. Somehow this professor had found out that we were scholarship athletes. I don't know how. Johnny went to confront it, although I don't know what the result was.

One thing we knew was that no one would know us by recognizing us from the games, because no one was coming to our games. In that regard, we had no problem keeping a low profile. In high school, I had played in games with fourteen thousand spectators; at Louisville, we had three thousand.

McDonald:

There wasn't a mean bone in his body . . . until he played football, and then he was all mean.

*Although Louisville couldn't be found on the major
college football map in those days, head coach Frank
Camp was well-known outside the school, as JOE
TRABUE remembers:*

Blanton Collier and Paul Brown were good friends of Coach
Camp's. Blanton would come and visit Coach Camp to see
what he was doing. They thought Coach Camp had one of
the best football minds of anyone in the country, and Coach
Camp convinced me that was true.

We had a solid running game, and there were some
things we did that drew the interest of Collier and Brown.
One was a play that we ran that was a pitchout involving the
halfback flaring, a rainbow pattern to his side, and the quarterback almost blindly making a quick reverse pivot and
tossing the ball to that halfback. If the defensive end made a
standard move, one step, the halfback had him beaten
already. That play then put the halfback on a defensive halfback, one on one, creating a lot of pressure on the defense,
and that was a play we ran very effectively.

The other thing we did really well was trap. It takes a lot
of practice to develop good trapping technique. That's how
we had been able to tie a very good Miami team in 1950.
When teams played us, we were so efficient that we could
run on almost any team out of the typical wide-tackle-six
defense in those days.

*FRANK OTTE, who played center on offense, remembers
Unitas's last game at Louisville, a 20–6 loss at Eastern
Kentucky that capped a 3–6 season in 1954:*

I can remember our last game together, his senior year, when
he was about to hang up the jockstrap for the last time. I

asked John what kind of work he was going to do for a living now, because it had never really dawned on me that he might want to play professional ball. He said, "I'm going to be a professional football player," and I said, "Well, I'll be damned. Good luck to you." The look he gave me. . . . I had never really seen that much in him to think he could play pro football, but then, the center never does get to see much going on behind and around him, other than the line play.

Behind the scenes, Camp and his staff at Louisville were hard at work trying to get some attention from NFL coaches for their players, most notably the relatively unknown Unitas. **CLARK WOOD:**

We knew one of the assistant coaches on Paul Brown's staff with the Cleveland Browns, and at one point they called Coach Camp about John. Coach gave John the highest recommendation he could give any quarterback. He tried to talk the Browns into taking him, but they ended up not doing it, and the Pittsburgh Steelers ending up drafting John in the ninth round.

A few years later, after John had made it big with the Colts, Paul Brown called Coach Camp and told him that next time he gave one of his players such a high recommendation, he (Brown) would not only give that player an opportunity to play with the Browns, but he would have to prove he didn't have the ability to play before they would ever think of cutting him. Coach Brown said, "I should have listened to you, but I didn't."

Just like he had done at Louisville, as soon as John got the opportunity, in Baltimore, he took right over, and that was it.

The Steelers' pick of Unitas was more a P.R. stunt than anything for the local boy. When he got there, he found three quarterbacks in front of him, and he saw very little action in training camp. Basically, they didn't know what to do with him. Hear it from **John Unitas** *himself:*

Most of the time they acted like I wasn't there. When I did get into an intrasquad scrimmage, I thought I played well. But I guess nobody was watching. Anyway, I was with them through five exhibition games, and they never put me in for a minute. Not a minute.[4]

Unitas, *again:*

I don't think Coach (Walt) Kiesling knew I was in camp—literally—until the AP (Associated Press) put out a picture of me showing a Chinese nun how to hold a football.[5]

Joe Trabue *had written many letters on John's behalf to NFL teams appealing for a chance for Unitas:*

When Johnny went to the Steelers, they wanted to put him on defense. As it was, there's no way that Johnny had the foot speed to be a defensive back in the NFL. It's no wonder Johnny was let go.

Shirley Green, *John's younger sister:*

John got married during his senior year in college, and it was tough for him not making it in pro football at first. So he got a job pile driving and then he played sandlot football. Those games were brutal. There was glass, tin cans, and a lot of other stuff all over that field on which they played. It was a horrible field to play on, which was in Lawrenceville.

John's getting cut by the Pittsburgh Steelers was awful for him, even though he didn't talk about it much. He was really depressed. They never really gave him a chance. There was a guy there named Vic Eaton, who was one of the other quarterbacks, and he ended becoming a defensive back.

JACK BUTLER was a Steelers defensive back who befriended Unitas in training camp in 1955:

He didn't get much attention to begin with, and once (Ted) Marchibroda came back, you knew they weren't going to keep him.[6]

ART ROONEY JR., son of the Steelers owner:

The coaches would run the quarterbacks through drills, and sometimes the whistle would blow before John even got a turn.[7]

After the Steelers had played their final preseason game, **JACK BUTLER** rode with Unitas back to camp:

He told me, "I think they're going to cut me." I said, "I don't think so. They can't cut you until they give you a shot." They cut him the next day.[8]

RON PETRELLI, who had played high school ball with Unitas, sometimes wonders what would have happened had John not been given a second chance, this time with the Baltimore Colts:

The Pittsburgh Steelers used John as cannon fodder before getting rid of him. If it hadn't been for the Baltimore Colts, I don't know what would have happened to him. Maybe he would have ended up being the greatest pile driver in the history of Pittsburgh, or the greatest whatever, maybe a phys. ed. instructor in one of the local school systems.

It was never a given that Unitas would make it with the Colts, as FRANK GITSCHIER recalls:

We had played against Weeb Ewbank when he was coaching at Washington University in Saint Louis. He had later gone to Baltimore to coach the Colts, and one time Weeb had called Coach Camp to find out more about Unitas. "What about this kid Unitas?" he said. "I don't understand; the Pittsburgh Steelers people said he was dumb and that he couldn't learn the playbook." We told him, "Hey, this kid can play."

So Weeb tells Don Kellett, the Colts' general manager. So they called John up, and for a ninety-cent phone call he ended up in Baltimore. After George Shaw got hurt, it's history.

After being cut by the Steelers, Unitas stayed home in Pittsburgh to find work. He was now married to Dorothy, his first wife, and they were about to become parents. FRED ZANGARO, another Pittsburgh native who had played at Louisville, helped Unitas put some of the pieces back together by helping him find a job and

University of Louisville Sports Information Department

Unitas often returned to his alma mater to help with charitable functions, and he was always mobbed by fans whenever he was in town. Here, he is surrounded by well-wishers during a Cardinals home game at which he was honored.

getting him to play for the Bloomfield Rams, a local sandlot semipro team. Zangaro:

I was a freshman at Louisville when John was a senior, but I was older than him because I had spent some time in the service during the Korean War.

I had to go home to Pittsburgh because I had a family to support and needed to get a job. About the same time John had been cut by the Pittsburgh Steelers. He had sent some letters to other teams and nothing had come through, so I asked him to come over to play for the Bloomfield Rams. I got paid three bucks a game, but John was better, so he got six dollars.

At Louisville, I had lived in a house with my wife and kid, and John would come out to have supper with us on Sundays, usually spaghetti and meatballs.

Coming out to play for the Rams would allow him to stay in shape and pick up a few bucks on the side, so it wasn't a bad situation for him. He realized that it was true. However, he still needed a job. My brother Dom got him working as a pile driver. We would work all day and then go to practice.

That field we played our games on was as hard as a rock, and there was always some glass on it. We would get some nice crowds for our games, before television ruined everything.

Chuck "Bear" Rogers was the owner as well as the coach and starting quarterback for the Rams. **ZANGARO:**

Chuck was about five seven and weighed about 230 pounds, and he wanted to be the quarterback because he owned and coached the team. Once he moved John to quarterback, though, John took charge of the team. We won the championship that year, and we won it again the next year without John, which goes to show that we had some pretty good personnel.

Our strength was our defense. There wasn't a whole lot of scoring, and John managed to get us at least a couple of touchdowns a game. What made us so good is that we had a legitimate offensive threat in John, and he could throw the ball.

Other teams would refer to him as a professional quarterback, because he had tried out for the Steelers, even though they cut him. But what was he supposed to do? When guys got cut by the pro teams and couldn't play anywhere else, they went to play for the semipro teams. I played for various teams up until 1967.

CHUCK ROGERS *explains how things worked with the Rams:*

We were just starting our season when Johnny got cut, and we were one of the few teams that were paying our players, although we weren't paying much. We had a couple of street fairs to raise some money.

Some players made six dollars a game, some made ten, and a few made fifteen. I think we had already played our first game when John came to the team, and we started him out at six bucks a game. We went and won the championship that year with seven or eight wins and one tie.

We practiced at night under the lights of the Bloomfield Bridge, and we played our games at Arsenal Field. It was a clay field that had to be oiled down—otherwise, when the wind was blowing, it would blow dirt and dust all over the place. That was bad because of all the people in the neighborhood who would be drying their clothes out on their clotheslines.

It was actually a junior high school field, with concrete bleachers on one side of the field. We used to rent the field and charge spectators three or four dollars a game. We would get a couple thousand people at our games. That's not much, though, compared to some of our high schools around here. High school football is pretty popular around here, and some schools will get ten or twelve thousand people a game.

We had a deal where if you were the visiting team, the home team had to give you five hundred bucks a game. Some of the teams couldn't afford it, so those games would be transferred to our field. So we played a lot of home games on that field.

ROGERS *remembers how the Bloomfield Rams had started out years earlier as something smaller:*

We started out when we were young, about thirteen or fourteen years old. The community in which I lived, Bloomfield, had a team on every street. Later on we got organized and pooled ourselves into one team, and we headed into the Honus Wagner League. As we grew older, we went into what they called the Steel Bowl Conference, where there were no age or weight limits, like a semipro league. Then we got teams from other communities. Eventually, the competition got pretty good. We started drawing from some former college players, even a few former pros.

RON PETRELLI:

The sandlot football was pretty good caliber.

CHUCK ROGERS:

It was semipro football, but not something I would call topnotch. We were a community team, about half of which was composed of guys who actually lived right in our neighborhood. We had players from schools like Wake Forest, Maryland, and Kent State.

There were a few teams that got into the league that came from smaller communities eighty or ninety miles away, but they weren't too competitive.

ROGERS *said he had no problem in handing over the starting quarterback's job to Unitas:*

John didn't exactly beat me out to become our quarterback. I gave him the job. I wasn't blind. After that, I just kicked extra points.

He made a pretty good impression, not just with his teammates but with our opponents as well. He was always a target for opposing players. They had written John up in the local papers as an ex-Steeler for crowd appeal, and he had an X written on his back because of it.

They used to beat him up pretty good. In fact, at Arsenal, the concrete wall was only about six or eight feet from the sidelines. They would throw him into that wall quite often, but he never lost his cool. I don't think I ever heard him swear or get into an argument with anybody.

John also played in our secondary. He'd never come out. He played every minute of every game.

FRED ZANGARO:

We didn't have a playbook or anything like that. We would just have some basic plays that we practiced and each one was given a name that John would then call in the huddle during games. John would even stoop down and draw a play in the dirt, perhaps showing a receiver how to run a certain pass route or whatever.

Our practices weren't greatly organized, but we managed to put a good team together and play well in games.

CHUCK ROGERS *was one of those who played a role in Unitas eventually getting a look-see from the Colts:*

John was kinda mad when he got to us after being cut by the Steelers. Baltimore was so bad, they used to have tryouts every Saturday. I sent a letter to their general manager, Don Kellett, telling him about another guy on our team, Jim Deglau, and he wrote me back a letter saying he was looking for this guy named Unitas.

So Unitas and Deglau both went to Baltimore, even though Unitas didn't really want to go. At the time, he was still being considered by the Bears and the Browns, and he was afraid that if he failed in Baltimore, it would hurt his chances of getting picked up by somebody else. But on his way to Baltimore, Otto Graham came out of retirement for the Browns.

John made a pretty good impression on the Colts, and they invited him back for the following year.

ROGERS continues:

John called all the plays for the Bloomfield Rams. You could always tell when he was going to pass because on pass plays John would keep one of our halfbacks, Red Culender, back to block and this guy would have steam coming out of his nostrils. He was steamed because he didn't want to be blocking; he wanted to be running the ball or going out for a pass.

On Saturdays, some of my players would sneak over to Baltimore for tryouts on Saturday because they knew Unitas was going to be going there the next year. In fact, the first year Unitas played for Baltimore, I had a punter named Woody McDaniel, who was really, really good. The Colts were having a lot of trouble with their punter. Unitas had told them about Woody McDaniel.

Finally, the Colts called Woody up. His dad was in the insurance business and had money, even his own airplane. The Colts offered him eight hundred bucks a game for two games. Woody called me and asked me what to do, and I said, "You're only making six bucks a game here, so going there even for nothing would be a good deal for you."

Well, he stalled around and stalled around, and this was at a time when I think you had to be in a city at least seventy-two hours ahead of time to be eligible to play. But the Colts had bad weather and left town a day early for a trip to the West Coast. Late in the game that Sunday, the Colts were protecting a small lead deep in their own territory, when their punter gets off a bad punt that puts San Francisco in position to score the winning touchdown, which they did.

After that McDaniel called them up for a tryout, and they wouldn't talk to him.

<hr />

Although the caliber of football the Bloomfield Rams played was well below NFL standards of the day, perhaps even a tad lower than what Unitas had experienced at Louisville, there was more to this semipro stuff than just rolling out the footballs and strapping on the pads. **CHUCK ROGERS:**

We ran from the T formation, the Oklahoma T, based on a book by Bud Wilkinson that we had gotten our hands on. We had been one of the first teams to use a man in motion and the split-T.

I had played quarterback for the main reasons of settling arguments in the huddle, to keep the peace. There were some guys that had to have their assignments reviewed for them in the huddle. We were also one of the few teams in the country to have two one-armed guys playing for us. One was a center and one was a guard.

We had a pretty good defensive team. There were some other good teams around, but not as good as us. I was always

Unitas in his later years, getting ready to be introduced at a University of Louisville game.

getting good new material. We were paying those few dollars a game, and that was attractive for some of the better players coming out. But I would get about half the money back because I would fine guys for missing practice.

We practiced four times a week, and played our games on Thursday nights. We practiced Monday, Tuesday, and Wednesday nights, and we would cancel Friday practice if we won on Thursday. One way or another, we practiced football pretty much year round because not many of the guys were interested in basketball or baseball.

FRED ZANGARO:

We had three officials calling our games, and there wasn't anything much in the way of dirty play. There was more sportsmanship than you see now. No fights or anything like that, although things started getting kind of wild starting in the late sixties, with cheap-shot artists and calling other guys bad things with profane language. We didn't have that back in the fifties.

ZANGARO also recalls the set of wheels Unitas drove, the image indelible on his mind:

John drove a green '41 Plymouth that he called the Green Hornet. It was an ugly green, but it was in pretty good shape.

One night right after Unitas had made it big with the Colts, he was out driving around in his car, when another car pulled up alongside his at a traffic light. Unitas looked over and recognized Steelers owner Art Rooney Sr. sitting in front and Steelers coach Walt Kiesling in the back seat. ART ROONEY JR. was there, too:

One of my brothers was driving, and he started talking to Unitas. After they pulled away, my father said, "Who was that?" When he heard it was Unitas, he asked my brother to catch up to him. At the next light, my father called out, "Hey, Unitas!" John said, "Oh, hi, Mr. Rooney." And my dad said, "I hope you become the greatest football player in the world." Then my dad turned around and gave Kiesling a dirty look.[9]

Author WILLIAM GILDEA, describing Unitas from his sandlot football days:

He wore number twenty-two on what was an odd-looking uniform to say the least. It had red-and-black-striped sleeves and a white front—that part was modeled after the University of Pennsylvania football jerseys of the time. But his helmet was scratched and dented—the last one to be given out. And his pants didn't reach his knees because they belonged to a friend several inches shorter. This was how John Unitas looked in the fall of 1955 when he played sandlot football in Pittsburgh for the Bloomfield Rams.[10]

JOHN UNITAS, *on playing for the Rams for just a few bucks a game after the Steelers had cut him and before the Colts grabbed him:*

I don't think any of them have ever understood that what mattered the most . . . was not the six dollars but the fact that there was a football team that wanted me.[11]

3

THE BALTIMORE COLTS

When the Pittsburgh Steelers cut Unitas in 1955, a local newspaper reported the move as involving a certain "Jack Unitas." By now it was clear that if he was going to make a name for himself, it would have to be somewhere other than Pittsburgh. That place turned out to be Baltimore, a city whose identity would come to be forever interwoven with the name Johnny Unitas. Think of one, and the other comes to mind.

A year after the Steelers cut Unitas, the Colts, acting on a letter recommendation, gave Unitas the genuine tryout he had been seeking in the first place with the Steelers. Unitas made the team as backup quarterback to George Shaw, the NFL's 1955 rookie of the year, and he took Shaw's place when Shaw tore up a leg in the fifth game of the 1956 season against the Chicago Bears. Shaw would never get his starting job back.

In going to the Colts, Unitas was joining a franchise that hadn't had a winning season in its nine years of existence. Once Unitas got his chance to play, the early results were not promising. When he replaced Shaw against the Bears, the Colts were ahead, 14–10. His first pass was intercepted and returned for a touchdown. On the next play from scrimmage, Unitas collided with running back Alan Ameche on a handoff and fumbled. Recovery and subsequent touchdown to the Bears. Unitas later botched another handoff, and, again, the Bears recovered and then scored en route to a 58–27 victory over the Colts.

It got better. Colts head coach Weeb Ewbank stuck with Unitas, who directed the Colts to a 4–4 record the rest of the season. The next year, 1957, the Colts finished with their first-ever winning record, at 7–5. The best was yet to come.

Author **WILLIAM GILDEA** interviewed Unitas for his book When the Colts Belonged to Baltimore, and with some background from others, pieced together how Unitas ended up with the Colts:

Unitas was living with his in-laws (in Pittsburgh). In February 1956 a three-minute toll call from Baltimore to Pittsburgh was eighty cents; hence, the legend that all it cost the Colts to get Unitas was an eighty-cent phone call. Unitas was at work when the call came, and Dorothy waited anxiously for John that evening to tell him the news. He took it with a characteristic shrug. He hadn't thought about Baltimore.

He was making $125 a week with overtime (on a pile-driving crew) . . . flitting out of town for another football tryout went against everything about work and family responsibilities that had been ingrained in Unitas. But Dorothy encouraged him to try Baltimore. And so he

A young Unitas, by this time in Baltimore, shows off some of his hard-earned hardware.

accepted (Colts General Manager Don Kellett's) invitation to come down for a one-day workout in May.

A few days later the mail brought what would be Unitas's first "National Football League standard players contract," which he signed and returned. If he made the club he would receive "the sum of $7,000 to be payable as follows: 75 percent of said salary in weekly installments commencing with the first and ending with the last regularly scheduled League game played by the Club during such season and the balance of 25 percent of said sum at the end of said last regularly scheduled League game."[1]

No one could have known it at the time, but the pieces were starting to come together to make the Colts into

one of the most enduringly great teams of the late
fifties and the sixties. All the years of hard work,
sacrifice, and toiling for overlooked schools was about
to pay off for Unitas. One of his Colts teammates was
split end **RAYMOND BERRY,** *who had gotten to the*
team a year ahead of Unitas. Their pairing would
eventually become legendary. Berry:

I got to the Baltimore Colts in the training camp of 1955. I
made it with the Colts, but in the course of the year I caught
only thirteen passes. Meanwhile, John that same year got cut
by the Steelers after six or seven weeks, so when we both
arrived at Colts training camp in the summer of 1956, we
were pretty much in the same boat—still-unproven players
getting a second chance.

Even though I was coming back to the Colts, I was slated
to be replaced. So with Johnny and me, you had two guys
just trying to survive. There's Johnny, an unknown free
agent, and me, a twentieth-round draft pick. We were both
desperate people. They had drafted an All-American receiver
as well as picked up another former All-American receiver
who had played two years in Canada, so I knew I was fighting for my roster life.

For training camp, John came in early with the rookie
group and I came in about a week later. Standing at the top
of the field at Westminster, Maryland, looking over the
sunken field there, somebody told me about this new quarterback we had gotten, a free agent from Louisville. Nobody
really knew who he was.

As I look back on that training camp now, I know it was
a very significant and unusual thing that was happening.
Weeb Ewbank, our head coach, was one of the most tremendous football coaches ever, a man who could recognize talent and teach football, and there have been very few coaches

who could do both well. Weeb had recognized something in John Unitas. Over the next six or seven weeks, Weeb would say to me, "Work with Unitas after practice, and keep working together."

Our starting quarterback was George Shaw, who had come with me in the rookie class of the year before. George had had a really good year, good enough to be Rookie of the Year in the NFL. He was the starting quarterback, but it didn't take long to know that Weeb just had this special feeling about Unitas. I knew this by the way he kept encouraging me to work with John.

As we went into the 1956 season, after we had both made the team, I can look back on it now and realize that Ewbank had made a decision on the both of us based on very little on-field production. I ended up beating out those other two newly acquired receivers to be named the starter at wide receiver, but we were a young team, too, so it's not like I was having to beat out a bunch of veterans, too.

Unitas went into the season as the backup to George Shaw, who a little ways into the season injured his knee badly in a game against the Bears. John came into the game, and that was to be his first NFL action. I don't know how many people remember this, but John's first completed pass as an NFL quarterback went for a fifty-six-yard touchdown to J. C. Caroline, who was a Chicago Bears defensive back.

ANDY NELSON, *a Colts defensive back, saw Unitas as the antithesis to what George Shaw brought to the table. As it turned out, Shaw would never be able to win back his starting job from Unitas:*

John was cool under pressure, and he had a good arm. He knew where the ball was going, and he was a great reader of defensive coverages. Shaw was more of a scrambler. He could run faster than John, but Weeb preferred a pocket passer, and that was Johnny. John could run when he had to, even though he didn't look that good doing it.

With Raymond Berry, you probably could have blindfolded John and he would always know where Berry would be on any given play. But that was possible because of their many hours of practice.

*After Unitas's first NFL pass was intercepted and returned for a touchdown, **RAYMOND BERRY** was eager to see how he would react:*

To give you a clue as to what made this guy tick, something which I didn't recognize fully until a few years later, in the huddle, after the interception, John just went about his business, unfazed by what had happened, and he went on to have a pretty decent day. From that point on, the Colts and Unitas started really mounting a tremendous passing attack.

Here's a guy who had been a free agent, desperate for a job, a backup quarterback with no NFL experience, and he throws his first pass for a touchdown going the other way. For a lot of guys, that could have been the end for them. What you didn't understand then, but which you know now looking back on it, is that Johnny's greatest trait was his mental toughness. He was a tough SOB, and he had tremendous confidence in his ability.

When he came off the field, he didn't kick the dirt or throw his helmet, or anything like that. He was never demonstrative anyway. He just went about his business, and it didn't shake him.

One thing I learned later as a coach myself, to give you a clue about this, I started coaching in the NFL because Tom

Landry talked me into it. I really didn't want to go into coaching, but he influenced me to do it, and I joined his staff in Dallas in 1968. Second year I was there, Roger Staubach came out of the navy as a twenty-seven-year-old rookie.

Roger's confidence coming into the league was very much like Unitas's had been in 1956. He believed in himself, and it was clear to me from having worked with him those first few weeks in training camp that he was going to be the starting quarterback for the Cowboys. We had our first rookie scrimmage game against the Washington Redskins rookies, and I saw what happened to Roger when he came up against the pro defenses, with more speed and quickness and athletic ability than he had ever faced before.

Roger didn't do that well. When I saw him after that, he was obviously rattled. It had shook him. Years later, I thought, if Roger Staubach, a mature twenty-seven-year-old man who had already commanded troops in Vietnam, and who was one of the most confident people I had ever been around, if he gets shaken, what is the average NFL rookie quarterback going to be like? Then I think back to Unitas as a rookie and how unshaken he had been after such a bad start, and I realize that that is what made Unitas Unitas.

*Unitas and Berry weren't the only ones trying to make the Colts in 1956; so was **LENNY MOORE**, a halfback about to learn the ropes as a flanker. Not only would all three make the big club and stay there a long time, all would eventually be enshrined in the Pro Football Hall of Fame at Canton, Ohio. Moore:*

Johnny U and I came to Baltimore in 1956. I came right after the College All-Star Game, and I met up with the team when they were in Hershey, Pennsylvania, to play an exhibition game with the Eagles. I hadn't heard of Unitas because there wasn't much to have heard about. He was just another member of the ball club—nothing to whoop and shout about. Yet. He was just seeking a job like I was.

John had been one of those sandlot players the year before, and the Colts brought in a lot of those guys to give them the once-over, just to make sure they might not be missing somebody good. You never know; in the midst of that could be that diamond in the rough, like Unitas.

George Shaw was our quarterback at that time, and George had all the tools of what most pro teams were looking for—a quarterback who was versatile, who could pass as well as run, someone who could keep a defense off balance, and George was excellent at that. I was too busy fighting for my own job to see who was doing what in other positions.

MOORE explains that there was a learning curve to deal with, fashioned by head coach Weeb Ewbank:

Weeb had an idea that he wanted all of his halfbacks to learn the wide-receiver positions. His thinking was that we never wanted to catch ourselves short personnel-wise. We had only about thirty-three guys on the team. So all of the running backs had to learn how to run pass patterns, just in case.

I didn't know anything about running pass routes. At Penn State we very seldom passed the ball. After a period of time, I became both a running back and a flanker, pretty much interchangeable.

Given Ewbank's emphasis on passing, **RAYMOND BERRY** and John Unitas took to heart the coach's

*suggestion that they work together after practice to get
their timing and routes down. Berry:*

We spent so much time talking and rehearsing that I think
we could almost read each other's mind on the field. It took
me thirty years to comprehend one of the great pay-offs from
all of this, from what happened in the 1958 sudden-death
championship game (the NFL Championship Game in
which the Colts beat the Giants in overtime, 23–17).

In the most crucial time of the game, perhaps on the
most important play of the game, it was in the two-minute
drive when we were behind and needed a field goal to tie.
We were some seventy yards away with no timeouts left.
John called a play in the huddle, a ten-yard square-in pattern
to me. We broke the huddle and came to the line. Harland
Svare, the Giants' outside linebacker, walked right out and
up to my face. Well, you're not going to run a ten-yard
square-in with a 250–pound linebacker around your neck.

The clock's moving and we don't have any cell phones or
radio earpieces in our helmets in those days. I look at John and
he looks at me, and he knew what we were going to do. It
wasn't exactly telepathy, but it was an understanding that we
had already created. We created this square-in pattern to a
slant. I gave an outside fake in order to try and get the linebacker to come after me, which he did, then I jumped under-
neath him, and John drilled me with the ball about six or seven
yards deep. We picked up thirty yards on the play, and we were
never in the huddle again after that because of the time factor.

So we go straight to the line of scrimmage, and he hit me
with another one; then we go to the line again, and he hit me
on another one. Then I get tackled inside the twenty, and the
clock's running. The offense runs off the field and the field-
goal team runs on and kicks the field goal to tie the game
with seven seconds left.

Weeb Ewbank, Unitas's first head coach with the Colts, goes over some plays with Unitas and backup quarterback George Shaw prior to the 1958 NFL Championship Game against the New York Giants.

Over our first three seasons together, John and I had often talked about what we would do in certain situations. Periodically, we would go over these things and rehearse them, such as what to do when we had called a square-in and then faced a linebacker out. I'm almost positive that leading up to the game, John and I had never discussed this particular scenario, but I do know that the Giants had never shown this kind of adjustment. So at that particular stage, when the clock is ticking and all the chips are on the line, this situation came up and we executed the adjustment. It was a one-time deal but typical of the payoff from the intense preparation we had together.

BERRY, *on Weeb Ewbank:*

One of the approaches that Weeb brought to the initial teaching of his passing offense was his emphasis on the short passing game. Also, we weren't holding on to the ball long—John was getting back there and getting rid of it.

One of the ways in which we helped change Weeb's mind, and it took about four years after I had proved myself to him, was to get him to realize that we were overbalanced on throwing the ball short. The defenses knew it, and we needed to be able to go deep. Weeb had always regarded the long pass as a poor-percentage play, but I helped convince him that we could execute this thing and that we would not abuse the privilege. He said okay.

We started going with the long ball and it made defenses more honest. We started getting some more of the things we wanted. It was a dimension to having a balanced offense that needed to be added.

The other thing Weeb was very leery about was throwing the ball inside. Over a period of time, we also convinced him that we had to do that. The reason is simple: It's the principle of balance. Just like in the running game, where you want to do more than just run between the tackles. That doesn't do a whole lot of good. Same thing with the passing game. You want the defense to know that you're perfectly capable of throwing the ball inside, outside, short, deep, etc. The message to the defense is, "You may be able to stop some of those, but you aren't going to stop all of them." That's what we had to convince Weeb about.

People had a misconception about the deep passing attack we had in Baltimore. I once had a guy write something about me that referred to me as just a "possession receiver." But the facts don't bear that out. As Weeb began to relax things about throwing the ball long, we started hitting some long balls. Any time you establish the short balls, you have some tremendous long balls just waiting for you. Fake the short one and go deep, and you can get some big chunks. But we were careful about not trying to get rich quick.

*Unitas proved himself a good fit and strong leader after taking over for George Shaw about a third of the way into the 1956 season, but he was no overnight sensation. That first year he completed 55.6% of his passes for 1,498 yards, nine touchdowns, and ten interceptions as the Colts struggled to a 5–7 finish. A year later, Unitas's numbers improved, respectively, to 57.1%, 2,550 yards, twenty-four touchdowns, and seventeen interceptions as the Colts finished 7–5. They were getting close, maybe just a player or two away from title contention. One of those missing pieces might have been **RAY BROWN**, a defensive back and backup quarterback drafted in 1958. Brown:*

They were looking for another piece to the puzzle and I was the only rookie starter on that team. I also did the punting, was also one of the backups to John at quarterback, and held the ball on extra points and field goals.

My third year I roomed with John on the road, after they had traded off George Shaw. For the next two years we were roomies. It was a tradition with Weeb, and probably for other teams, too, for position players to room together on the road.

We never did anything really exciting on the road. We would fly in the day before, check into the hotel, have a light workout, go back to the hotel and have maybe two or three hours free—no more, and then have what they would call an evening snack. There was a lot of food like big burgers as well as fruit. No beer.

There wasn't much time to go and fool around on these trips, except when we went to the West Coast. Those trips were usually more than a week. We would go out a few days early to L.A. to get acclimated, then head up to San Francisco for a week, then after that game get on a plane and fly all night back home.

When we did have some time, we might go walk around, do some shopping, maybe even go to a movie. It wasn't a rowdy kind of thing.

Once Unitas had established himself as the Colts' starting quarterback, his next quest was to get Ewbank to buy into the philosophy that Unitas should be calling the plays on the field. **LENNY MOORE** *often was within earshot of the two:*

Nobody was going to going to call the shots but Johnny. He proved he was capable of being able to handle that. The thing with him is, if you thought he was going to do something, he wouldn't do it; if you didn't think he would do something, he would. Unpredictable, and sometimes he would call things right off the wall. All he was doing was playing the defense, setting something up.

I would overhear them on the sideline, and Weeb would be asking John, "Do you think we ought to do this?" Or, "What do you think will work here?" And John would say, "Hell, Weeb, I don't know. What do you think?" It would always be that kind of conversation. Weeb knew John was capable of working it out. Weeb might send something into the huddle, and John would just disregard it and call whatever he was going to call.

As the years flew by, it eventually dawned on
RAYMOND BERRY *that these were special times:*

We spent twelve seasons together. What are the odds of
something like that happening? Believe me, it never got old.

Elroy Hirsch was my idol in those days and I would
dream of being able to make catches like ol' Crazy Legs. I
not only got to be a receiver in pro football, I also got to be
with the greatest quarterback. Then there was the idea of
being with such a great team.

Carroll Rosenbloom was the key man to all this. He was
an owner who set the tone, starting with the hiring of Weeb
Ewbank. Rosenbloom is the one who brought all this
together, and he was totally committed to winning on top of
all this.

Ewbank kept it simple, basic, and totally sound, and he
hardly ever missed on keeping players with talent. It was a
balanced team, with a great defense, a solid running game,
and good players at every position. Weeb was a master at
pass protection, so John was working in a situation where he
had maximum opportunity to do what he could do best.
And Weeb let Johnny use his instincts as a play-caller. Weeb
and John got along well.

John would talk to our offensive linemen; he would talk to
me. If I could get open, I would tell him. If I couldn't get open,
I would also tell him that so that we wouldn't waste plays.

Even if John were playing today, where plays are so programmed and the coaches on the sideline call almost all the
plays, a perceptive coach would realize what John had and
give him plenty of room to call his own plays. Any good
coach adjusts to his talent and can assess what his guys can
do and try to put them into situations where they can do
what they do best.

When I was coaching the New England Patriots and had Steve Grogan at quarterback, I had someone who was the smartest guy on the team and understood the offense. We had the best chance of moving the ball when he was calling the plays. These days I wonder what the Oakland Raiders are doing with Rich Gannon. I've got the feeling that they're giving Gannon a lot more input with the plays than the average quarterback gets. Ditto for the Colts and Peyton Manning.

It all came together for Ewbank, Unitas, and the Colts in 1958. In Ewbank's fifth season at the helm, the Colts finished 9–3 despite losing their last two regular-season games. They won the Western Conference, and then it was on to New York and Yankee Stadium for the 1958 NFL Championship Game against the New York Giants, champions of the Eastern Conference. **SAM HUFF**, *a Giants linebacker in those days, sets the scene:*

It was a great game. Two great ball teams in Yankee Stadium—you couldn't ask for anything better. John was the difference in the game.

One time I was at some function, and Artie Donovan was there, and he was carrying on about how great a team they had. He kept going on and on, and I let him go until he was finished. Then I said, "Artie, if it hadn't been for John Unitas, it would not have been close." He just shut up.

Unitas had all the confidence in the world and the nerve of a bank robber. He never lost control.

The first time I ever played against him had been up in Boston. George Shaw was their quarterback at that time, and we played against them in a preseason game. We rode trains in those days. Shaw didn't play in that game, but Unitas did and we beat them. I can remember riding back in the train

Unitas twice led the Colts to NFL Championship Game victories over the New York Giants, in 1958 at Yankee Stadium, above, and in 1959 at Baltimore.

after the game, and no one knew how to pronounce his name. We were calling him "YOU-nuh-tiss." Shaw was more of a running quarterback for them, although he ran scared, that's what he did. As for John, he just got better and better after that.

That 1958 championship game was a heckuva game, and they beat a really good team. We had the lead and couldn't hold it for the last two minutes. He kept throwing the ball to Berry and running the ball with (Alan) Ameche, and he did a masterful job of moving the ball down into field-goal territory. He was crafty. I would go help out on covering Raymond

Berry, and then Unitas would hand off to Ameche for seven yards or whatever up the middle. It was a classic two-minute drill. We were playing a bit looser because we thought we had the game won, and they had a lousy kicker besides.

Unitas was masterful and with Lenny Moore at flanker instead of coming out of the backfield, he had two great receivers to throw the ball to, and I'm telling you, he could really throw the football.

So it ended up tied, and then the referee came to us on the sideline and said, "Okay, we're going to take a three-minute break and then we're going to play sudden-death." We thought, *What the hell is that?* Nobody had even heard of sudden-death. We were just trying to figure out what was happening. You condition yourself to play a game, not to play five quarters. It was kind of tough, and then John really moved the ball in that overtime.

Tom Landry was our defensive coordinator. Landry was never baffled, and he knew that it was time to go back to the fundamentals when things went wrong: Do very simple things, which we did. We just thought we could stop them with execution alone. But John had a hot hand, and he just kept throwing the ball, zipping it in there.

One time it was third and ten, and he threw the ball to Raymond Berry, who broke a tackle and picked up a first down, right near the end of the game. That was a key play.

ANDY NELSON, *a Colts defensive back who was named to the 1960 Pro Bowl, also remembers being bewildered by the idea of playing overtime:*

I don't really know if it was the greatest game ever played, but it did propel the NFL to another level. I had never heard of overtime. When the game ended in a tie, we just started walking off the field, thinking the game was over. Then we got called back, and we were told that we were going to play it off. Sudden death? Never heard of it.

RAY BROWN:

One thing I remember about the 1958 game is Sam Huff afterward going, "Unitas to Berry, Unitas to Berry, Unitas to Berry." I also remember one play in which someone for the Giants caught a pass about fifteen yards downfield. One of us hit the guy and the ball popped loose. Everyone was scrambling for the ball, and it was a mad, Keystone Kops-type of thing. The ball just kept rolling and bouncing, and people were falling over themselves trying to get it. I don't remember who got it.

RAYMOND BERRY weighs in on the significance of the 1958 NFL Championship Game, which is still commonly referred to as the greatest game in league history:

We, the players, weren't really aware that we were a part of history or making history. After the game, outside the stadium on the sidewalk, I happened to see Bert Bell, who was then the commissioner of the NFL. I noticed that he had tears in his eyes. Years later, the significance of that moment started to dawn on me. He had been nursing that baby, and he understood immediately what that game had meant.

The NFL Championship Game in 1958 continues to get the headlines, but LENNY MOORE says it was a game a few weeks earlier that he remembers as key:

The greatest game we played as a team was a game against the San Francisco Forty-niners we played about a month prior to the championship game.

We were down 27–7 at halftime. They had Y. A. Tittle at quarterback, Joe Perry at fullback, and Hugh McElhanney at halfback. They also had John Henry Johnson, Billy Wilson, and there was big Bob Saint Clair on defense. How in the hell were we supposed to stop them from moving the ball?

At halftime, Weeb said, "We're going to go back out in the second half and score a touchdown right off. Then we're going to score again, again, and again. We're going to score four touchdowns." And that's what he wrote on the blackboard.

We got those touchdowns and ended up winning, 35–27. The defense tightened on those guys, and J. U. went to work. I mean, *J. U. went to work!*

ART DONOVAN, *the hulking tank of a defensive tackle who occasionally can still be spotted doing a guest spot on late-night television, had this to say in his book,* Fatso:

During the Forty-niners game in 1958 here in Baltimore, Unitas kept calling Lenny Moore's number in the huddle, and Moore kept slashing through the San Francisco defense. So after about half a dozen straight runs by Moore, Lenny came back to the huddle and told John, "Hey, man, cool it. I'm getting tired." Whooa. Nobody tells John Unitas to "Cool it." (Jim) Parker says Unitas's face turned into a flinty stare, and his eyeballs nearly burned a hole through Lenny's head. "Listen, [expletive], nobody tells me to cool it," Unitas said. "I'll run your [butt] till you die." He put the fear of God in him, and by this time Lenny's stammering, "Forget it, John. Forget I said anything. Give me the ball, please. Give me the ball on every play."[2]

The Colts and the Giants would return to the NFL Championship Game in 1959, this time in Baltimore, where the Colts again prevailed, 31–16. **SAM HUFF:**

Going to Baltimore, to play the old Colts, was like going to Green Bay: Home-field advantage in any big game is very important, particularly in Green Bay and Baltimore. Even now you got to Green Bay and you have your hands full.

After Unitas took over for George Shaw at quarterback, it didn't take him long to assert his authority in the huddle. But Unitas wouldn't stonewall his teammates when it came to input. **LENNY MOORE:**

John called me "Sput," short for Sputnik, which Big Daddy (Lipscomb) had given me in 1957 after the Russians launched Sputnik. In the huddle, he would say, "Sput, what have you got?" And I might say, "The slant is there, the slant takeoff is there, any time for the angle-in is good, at eight, ten, or twelve yards, whatever you want."

He still might not call the play, waiting for his own timing. Then all of a sudden, we would get in there and he'd say, "Okay, is it still there, Sput?"

"Whenever you're ready, my man."

Raymond (Berry) would always be bringing back stuff to him. "John, I can do a Q," or "John, I can do a slant takeoff." John would file that back in his head, go back to calling his own plays, and then bring that input back for a certain play

Sport magazine awarded Unitas a Corvette in naming him most valuable player of the 1958 NFL Championship Game, in which he led the Colts to a dramatic 23–17 overtime victory over the New York Giants.

in a particular situation. "Raymond, you still got it?" And that was it.

ANDY NELSON *roomed with Unitas on the road for a while:*

John was never nervous before a game. He slept well, and his concentration in the game the next day was great. All we would do the night before a game was go out and eat and maybe go to a movie. He didn't stay out late like some guys do. John didn't have any highs or lows—he was always just straight down the middle.

After winning the back-to-back titles in 1958 and 1959, the Colts would never again appear in a playoff game with Ewbank as coach. Ewbank would coach three more seasons, two of which ended up at .500 and the other at 8–6, in 1961. Don Shula took over as head coach in 1963, leading the Colts to seventy-one victories during his seven seasons there. The Colts would not win another league championship until the early seventies, but they had staying power through the sixties, contending for playoff spots almost every season and winning their share of those contests. **LENNY MOORE** *elaborates:*

In terms of reputation, I think we were shortchanged a bit when you compared us to the likes of the Green Bay Packers of the sixties and then the Pittsburgh Steelers or Dallas Cowboys of the seventies. We had won the championship in '58 and '59, but we were pretty much forgotten in the sixties even though we were always in the mix of things every year.

As great as that team was—and sometimes when I go over our roster I can't believe all the Hall of Famers we had there, at one time—there were no "stars;" no one thought of himself as a star, and that's the way we played. We were the Baltimore Colts.

You could attribute that to Don Kellett, our general manager, who made it a point that we would do as much as we could together, aside from the racial thing. In doing things for the community, the black players could do things in the black communities and their notoriety would transcend into the white community, but it would not work the other way around. Very seldom did you see the white guys on the team doing community work in the black areas of town.

*To help spice things up, the Colts in 1959 brought running back **ALEX HAWKINS** on board. Hawkins was an outgoing, talkative, nightlife-type of guy who would stick with the team for a few years and eventually end up working in a network-telecast booth as an analyst. Hawkins, who would become good friends with Unitas, his polar opposite in the area of personality, recalls how he came to the Colts:*

I was originally drafted out of South Carolina in 1959 by the Green Bay Packers—Lombardi's first year—as the thirteenth person taken in the draft.

Lombardi and I didn't get along at all, and, of course, he always got the last word. So I was gone, and the Colts picked me up on waivers, or at least in some kind of trade that involved nothing for something. I joined the Colts before their last preseason game. So, in effect, I went from having Bart Starr as my quarterback to John Unitas.

I had played one preseason game with the Packers. They had a policy in which they would start you for a half, and if you got pulled before the half was over, it meant you had performed poorly and were gone. Bart Starr and I started a game up in Portland—I don't remember who we were playing—but neither one of us performed well, and Lombardi took us out of the game.

I was sitting on a bench on the sideline, and there I am a rookie who knows nothing, and Bart is sitting there sniffling and crying. I said, "What the hell is wrong with you?" He said, "He took me out, he took me out." I said, "Damn, man, he took me out, too." But Lombardi went on to make Starr a man and a player.

HAWKINS *remembers what went through his mind*
when he first saw Unitas:

I thought he was the goofiest-looking guy; he looked like a
farm boy from Mississippi or someplace. Everything about
him was awkward: his mannerisms, his hair, even his hands.
He had a hump in his back when he stood, and his legs were
skinny. There just didn't seem to be anything athletic about
him. There never really *was* anything athletic about John: he
was just a *quarterback*, period.

Johnny Unitas's hallmark was the huddle. Nobody spoke
anything in the huddle, I don't care what it was. If you had
something to say to Johnny, you said it before you got into
the huddle, which was his cathedral. Even great players like
Lenny Moore and Raymond Berry acted like scared rookies
when it came to that huddle. You did not utter a word in
there unless Johnny specifically called on you.

You get that respect by delivering and demanding. He
delivered time and time again, far more often than not.

HAWKINS *also saw a cultural difference when he went*
from Lombardi's Packers to Ewbank's Colts:

It was nothing like the Packers. The Colts were individuals.
(Don) Shula allowed that, and so had (Weeb) Ewbank to a
degree. Shula's thing was "Work hard, play hard. Give me all
your effort when you're on the field, practice hard before a
game, and live your life the way you want to." As for
Lombardi, he preached fear and was more concerned about
your personal life as well.

I think having a little of that independence helped make
Johnny who he was. Johnny and Weeb got along beautifully,
but he and Shula did not get along as well. I think it was

more of a personality thing than anything else—it was a quiet, underlying kind of thing. They just tolerated each other. John's role was as leader of the Colts, and I suppose that can cause clashes with the coach.

Something not seen much anymore in sports is a nucleus of players that stays together for more than three or four seasons. Consider this: Unitas, Berry, and Moore all started for the Colts for eleven seasons, from 1956 through 1966. It's no wonder they became so familiar with each other, as well as their environs. One of the quirks of Memorial Stadium was an area on the right side of the closed end of the field, near where the Baltimore Orioles had their dugout. It could create havoc for opposing defenses, and Unitas knew it well, as wide receiver **JIMMY ORR** *explains:*

If you laid down in the middle of the field, it looked like it sloped a couple of yards downhill to that corner. I swear, that made me run faster. On Thursdays, we would practice at the stadium without the defense, and John and I would get our timing down. It was scary in that corner, tight. You go into a place where there are walls and people, subconsciously, that affects you, especially if you're a defensive back. We would go sliding into that baseball warning track, and I had a couple of cinders in my arm for a long time.[3]

A key acquisition for the Colts came in 1961, when they drafted quarterback **TOM MATTE** *out of Ohio State, where he had played for Woody Hayes. Matte would be converted to running back, eventually starting in 1963, but he was a good guy to have*

Andy Robustelli of the Giants pulls down Unitas in the 1959 NFL Championship Game, a rematch between the Colts and Giants played before a sellout crowd of 57,577 at Baltimore Memorial Stadium.

around at crunch time, such as filling in at quarterback when Unitas was injured prior to the 1965 Western Conference Championship Game. Matte talks about coming to the Colts, by 1961 a well-established club loaded with veterans:

I came to the Colts in 1961 as their number-one draft choice. I had to play in the All-Star game, so I got to camp about two weeks late. They were going to convert me over to a running back or a defensive back, so I wasn't even sure what my role was going to be.

There were high expectations of me because of where I had been drafted, and I think I was a bit of a disappointment. Normally, veterans don't have a whole lot of sympathy for the rookies at all. Then I got hurt, crushed a couple of vertebrae in my back in our opening game. So I had a lot of time to sit back and study what professional football was all about. When you're a rookie, you don't know anything.

It was a rude awakening, and John was instrumental in helping me adjust. He taught me how to study film and how to be able to read defenses. That's what really helped me over the years to stay with this ball club as a running back for twelve years, which is almost unheard of now. John had a lot of confidence in me because he saw I was putting a lot of time and energy into learning the game, like he did.

Coaches today measure players by how fast they are and how big they are. Back when we played, the coaches and the players both measured you by how smart you were and by what kind of heart you had. John knew I was a pretty smart football player and that I had the heart to play, that I loved the game of football, where a lot of guys are in it just for the money.

I even told my wife one day that the day I start playing for money and not for my love of the game would be the day I quit. And that's what I did after John and I got traded out to San Diego (after the 1972 season). They wanted John and me to go out there, initially, as player-coaches, and I would have been going only to pick up a paycheck. That didn't appeal to me. I had been a business major in college and wanted to put my degree to use. Woody Hayes, my coach at Ohio State, had made sure of that, that I would have a degree that would give me a fallback position once I got out of football.

I established myself in the community of Baltimore, and so this is where I stayed.

MATTE, *on what it was like playing for Hayes:*

Woody really looked after his players and made sure they graduated. I can remember my rookie year with the Colts, he called me three times during the season to remind me that I had eight hours of classes to make up to complete my degree. And he said, "I want your butt back here in Columbus to graduate."

When I walked off the podium with my degree, Coach Hayes was there to grab me and, turning to my mom, he said, "Mrs. Matte, I told you that your son would graduate from Ohio State, and he just did. My commitment to you is finished."

That's a great tribute to the man. He was a hard guy to play for—I didn't get along with him very well, but my respect for him grew as I matured. Sort of like my dad: I always thought he was the dumbest guy in the world, until I turned thirty and figured out he wasn't so dumb anymore.

MATTE, on Weeb Ewbank:

Weeb Ewbank was a very smart coach. He knew the game of football very well. On game days he was hyperactive, but he always had a great game plan. He had grown up under Paul Brown and he had a great system with practices all set up and with game plans presented the right way, offensively and defensively. He was very organized and taught me a lot.

When we got new coaches in, it would be pretty much up to me to teach them the system and the playbook. Basically, I would become their roommate for a while. John was more reserved and laid back, where I felt comfortable joking around with the coaches. I was the prankster, the fun guy to be around.

Every year, we would get new running backs in who would see me and think, *Slow, white halfback,* and all that stuff. And every year I'd be taking their playbook and saying,

"Good luck with your next team because Unitas really wants me in his backfield."

Basically, I owe my whole career to John Unitas because he and I had a great communication. He knew where I was going to be on every play. We came up with a play that we designed ourselves, which we called the halfback option. Coming out of the backfield, I could go inside or outside, and John would stay with me no matter what the linebacker did. If it was a zone, John would go toward the sideline; I would follow him out there and then hook in front of him, and he'd lay the ball out there for me.

The only way you could stop the play was by tackling the guy while he was coming out of the backfield. The only guy who could figure that out was Maxie Vaughan, a linebacker for the Rams who had played with the Colts. When I came out of the backfield, he would just tackle me instead of trying to cover me. He'd get called for holding every once in a while, but most of the time he got away with it. Nobody else did that.

MATTE *elaborates on the Unitas work ethic:*

I didn't seek him out when I first got to the Colts. I was scared to death. But you had to go to him if you wanted him to talk things over with you. If you wanted to work on something after practice, you had to go to him. When you told him what you wanted to work on, he would say, "Okay, let's go do it." He never went in until everyone was satisfied.

He was a workaholic, and Raymond Berry was the same way. Timing, timing, timing on all the pass patterns. They worked on that stuff all the time after practice. How many steps to take before a cut: three steps, two steps, six steps— the ball would be thrown on the dot. Two-point-one seconds, two-point-three, two-point-five. How many steps are you taking back, three, five, or seven? Everything was timing. He would release the ball when the guy is making his break, and John had to be smart enough to read whether or not the bait had been taken on a pattern to throw it to the outside, to the middle, or wherever.

John had great vision. He could see across the field as well as anybody I've ever known. He'd look strong side and see that the zone was rotating, taking a pass play away, and immediately he would come back to the weak side. That's where I came back, on the weak side, where he could just drop it off to me.

We always had a decent running game going because they were expecting the pass and dropping back. We could pick up some nice rushing yardage that way. If we were throwing the ball too much, John might come back into the huddle and say, "What do you guys need?" And they would say, "John, you gotta slow these guys down, they're coming around the corners too quickly. Run a screen or a draw, and then we can slow them down because they have to run a check first." So John would run a draw or screen, and it would work, keeping those defensive linemen from teeing off on us.

With Unitas in charge of the offense, there usually wasn't much to be uptight about—until Ewbank tried to get in on the action from the sideline. **Matte:**

With John calling the plays, we would sometimes have some funny situations with Ewbank on the sideline. I would be on the sideline, and it would be third down in a critical situation, and Weeb would grab me by the arm, push me on the field, and say, "Tell John to call this." I'd say, "What?" He'd pull me back and say, "Tell John to call . . . uh . . . uh. Okay . . . uh . . . tell John to get a first down."

I'd run into the huddle and, of course, John would get a first down or touchdown at some critical point. The papers the next day would say how Weeb Ewbank had sent the key play in. Truth is, when I got out there and walked into the huddle in that situation, John would ask, "What ya got?" I'd say, "The usual." He'd say, "Get a first down?" "Yeah."

On game day Weeb really left it all up to Unitas. There was a conflict later on because Shula wanted to take over a little bit. Shula liked to control more of the game, and John didn't want anything to do with it. He'd say, "You run the defense, I'll run the offense, and leave me alone." They meshed as best they could, but there was always an underlying tension there.

Shula and I got along great because I would joke with him and have some fun with him. If anybody ever questioned John about his football knowledge, he was on the defensive right away. Shula had played for a year or two with the Colts as a teammate of John's and then he comes back a few years later as the youngest head coach in NFL history. I even think the underlying tension between them might have been more on John's part than on Shula's. John wasn't real enamored with Don Shula.

DON SHULA, *on his relationship with Unitas:*

Although we were never close, I had a good, honest relationship with John. Becoming close to Unitas is something that only a few people have succeeded in doing. I have always respected John as a quarterback. When I got to know John, I respected him as a person, although he was a loner in every sense of the word. He, at times, was friendly and concerned

and interested in my thoughts as coach. Only a few times did
we ever exchange disagreeable words.[4]

TOM MATTE *talks about the time he subbed at
quarterback for the injured Unitas in 1965:*

I had never thought about it because I didn't think he would
ever go down. But I was thrown into that in 1965, which was
in the days when we kept only two quarterbacks. I had a
cheat sheet on my arm, the same way I got through college
(laughing), and I had the input of John.

My abilities were not like John, who was a pure passer,
so they designed an offense around my abilities, which was
rolling out, running the ball, and dumping it off—using the
running game, to include quarterback draws, to preempt the
passing game. Usually, it was the other way around, when
John was in there.

---

*Although reserved in demeanor, Unitas wasn't shy. He
spoke up when necessary, as he did during practice
leading up to the 1964 Pro Bowl. Take it away,* **LENNY
MOORE:**

I went to seven pro Bowls, and I'll never forget the one in
1964. We had Vince Lombardi as our coach. The two quarterbacks there were Unitas and Bart Starr.

One day we were sitting in a meeting deciding what we
were going to do at our practice to follow. Vince says,
"Boys, we're going to keep it simple, and we're going to
keep it short and right to the point. We're not going to do
anything intricate. We're just going to use the basic 4–3
defense.

"Offensively, let's keep it simple. On the right of the center, if we want to do a sweep, let's just say 'sweep right.' If we want to go the left, we say 'sweep left.' Short tackle right and short tackle left for off-tackle plays. Cross block means we're going to hit between the guard and the tackle. Quick hitter, right up the center. Does everybody have that?"

Then he goes on to give a few really basic pass plays, such as a couple of slants and a couple of square-ins, including some slant-ins just for me. That was it. He wanted me to work with Bart on timing some of that stuff he gave me, because he knew John and I already had it down pat.

There was one play that Lombardi set up whereby the tight end was on the right side, yet we were going to run either off-tackle or bounce it around the end—on the left side. He says, "We want this guard pulling so he can kick out the linebacker as our tight end tries to go around the linebacker and make it a stalemate. Does anybody have any problems with that?"

Unitas raises his hand.

"Yeah, John."

"Coach, where do you want the halfback lined up? I'm thinking that we can do it two ways. We can put the right halfback on the right-hand side and then put the fullback behind the quarterback."

Vince says, "Well, John, if we do that, we're showing our strength side."

"Well, Coach, the strong side is already showing because you have the tight end over there. Tell you what, why don't we take that tight end and flex him three or four yards out from the tackle, and this way we can isolate the tight end on the linebacker and be able to still do the pass or the run, where this way we are pretty tied down to just the run?"

Lombardi says, "John, we've been going over running plays, but I like that idea. We can do that. We can do that."

Remember, this is Vince Lombardi that John's talking to. Everybody else was just sitting there, not saying a word.

***

MOORE *didn't see much of a change in offensive strategy with the Colts after Shula took over from Ewbank:*

Shula used the same stuff that Ewbank did. After all, they both came out of the Paul Brown system. You could do a little bit of everything you wanted and make it as simple as you want or as difficult as you wanted to make it. But you could handle every situation confronted with without worrying about killing ourselves.

The key to all of that was having Johnny U because he did the unexpected. Everything had to be timed up, so that when John got back at three and two-tenths seconds and was ready to release, I had to have my pattern completed. The one no-no was "Don't cross me up," which all of us did to John at one time or another. Sometimes a guy would have great coverage on you, and you might break a pattern, and that would mess John up.

***

There were times that Unitas had no choice but to run with the ball. **RAY BROWN**:

John stood in that pocket, and when he ran it was almost straight ahead. It was planned that way, because if the pocket broke down, it usually broke down up the middle. He would make his yardage somewhere between the tackles.

He did pretty well. He wasn't fleet of foot. But you didn't see him running to the sideline to escape out of bounds, and back then quarterbacks didn't take those slides before getting hit like they do now.

I would wince sometimes seeing him get hit hard, knowing how valuable he was to us.

BROWN, *being a backup quarterback, would often hang around after practice to observe or even help out when Unitas and Berry were doing their thing:*

Berry had a big net strung up behind him when he was working after practice with John on their passing plays. Raymond fashioned this big frame to catch the ball when it got by him. When John got tired, he would have me take over throwing to him. Raymond would come from all angles, left to right, right to left, jump up, dive down—make us throw the ball in all kinds of ways.

He always made it a point to catch the ball with his hands, not into his body like you see a lot of people do. He would catch who knows how many balls after practice, just working on sure reception of the ball. He would also work time and time again on the timing, right down to the tenth of a second on carefully measured routes.

John was willing to stay after practice and work like this, but he would always ask me to hang around.

LENNY LYLES, *who played with Unitas at both Louisville and Baltimore, goes back in time to offer details about Unitas, the man and the quarterback:*

Even though I grew up in Louisville, I really didn't know who Johnny Unitas was. I just wasn't that knowledgeable about football. I was fast, strong, and had good size, and knew how to play the game. No one had really taught me much about football, except to just give me the ball and tell me to run.

As soon as I saw John play, I knew he was great because, first of all, he could throw the ball better than anybody else I had ever seen in my life, and he had some great skills. We had great respect for him, but he was about all we had in terms of experience.

I got to know him a lot better after we had both gotten to Baltimore. I'm not even sure if the Colts had all that much respect for John, because he was behind George Shaw when I got there. Then when Shaw got hurt and John took over at quarterback, I remember thinking, *All right, this is my big chance, because we have played together before and this will work in my favor.*

My first year with the Colts was that 1958 season in which we won the world championship in the first-ever overtime game. I don't remember a whole lot about that game, except that they wouldn't let me return kicks because they were afraid I might drop the ball. They weren't going to trust me with the ball in the championship game.

LYLES, *an African American, came into football when there still was a deep racial divide between blacks and whites, in and out of sports. He saw it when he got to the Colts in 1958, striving for a spot on the roster:*

We had about a half-dozen blacks on the team, and it was clear that they weren't going to have that many blacks on the team. That's just the way it was; you've got to understand the times.

It took me a while to blossom, and I think they kept me around because I had made a couple of nice kick returns. Unfortunately, there wasn't anybody who could reach me. They cut me the next year, and I ended up with the Forty-niners.

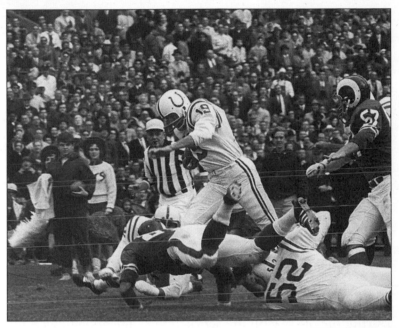

He wasn't known for his running or scrambling skills, but when the situation called for it, Unitas could tough it out on his own. Here he is running for paydirt in a 1965 game against the Los Angeles Rams.

I like to believe that I could have contributed more if I hadn't had to worry about all this other stuff, like not being able to eat in the same restaurants or, in some cases, stay in the same hotels as my teammates, or having to really fight to keep my position every time the team I was on drafted another black player at my position—then it would always between me and the other black player for that position, instead of between that black draftee and a white guy playing the same position.

I was green, I was impressionable, and I was a good athlete; all I needed was for somebody to grab me and help mold me into what I could be. When I went to San Francisco, I had a defensive coach in Jack Christenson, who had been a defensive back with the Detroit Lions. He told me, "I'm going to make a defensive back out of you," and I said, "I can't play defensive back."

Jack got ahold of me, bolstered my confidence, and turned me into a DB. I ended up playing defensive back and returning kicks, and in 1960 I ran back two kickoffs for touchdowns against the Colts, and we beat them. In 1961, the Colts brought me back. I was available because the Forty-niners had too many defensive backs ahead of me and no longer had room for me.

I was a different creature when I got to the Colts this time—nasty, ugly, vengeful. In practice, I acted like they weren't even my teammates. One time I got into it with Raymond Berry, but he took an interest in me anyway. He knew I had good speed, but I didn't have good hands. During the off-season, he worked with me and showed me what to do, making a lot of time for me. What he did for me was prolong my pro career.

John didn't have the time to nurse me along—he had a whole team to lead, and I certainly couldn't expect him to drop everything else to help me along. Raymond and some other guys helped me along, and I think they realized that with my speed, I could really help them, once someone showed me how to get open and how to do a better job of catching the ball.

LYLES, *on the issue of race, and on getting to know*
Unitas:

John was a special guy. Our friendship never developed to the point where I would share my inner feelings with him much—we didn't have time for it. Years later, after we had both retired, I told him, "John, I hate that I didn't help you as much as I could have. I was so busy with trying to protect myself, of trying to find my place, of being so consumed with me and my surroundings, that I never was able to figure out how I could help you." He looked at me kind of funny when I told him that, and I think he understood what I was trying to say. At least I hope he did.

I didn't have the character of a Lenny Moore, who was someone who could play well and play with discipline, even with all this racial stuff going on around him. I didn't have this problem at Louisville, where I was just given the ball and told to run. Then when I got to the pros, there was a certain level of distrust toward me. Nonacceptance. I wanted it, badly, but I couldn't get it the way that I wanted it.

I remember one time in the pros during a practice, when I went out for a pass. Everyone on offense stood up with hands on hip to see if I would catch it, and all the guys on defense turned around as well to watch. Talk about pressure. I'd be thinking, *Oh, please, Lord, let me catch this one.*

It was my responsibility to learn how to catch the ball, and I had to learn how to be able to turn my head correctly to look for the ball. Lenny Moore was different—he was great, he already knew how to do all this stuff. That slant play we used to run—man, that ball would come at you at a hundred miles an hour. I was fast, I could run, but my hand-and-eye coordination wasn't that good.

ALEX HAWKINS recalls one of many times that Unitas would just hang in there and keep playing, even when badly hurt:

Every time we played the Chicago Bears it was a war, and I remember one time in particular when we were playing them up in Chicago. We would get beat physically or on the scoreboard, or both.

This one happened to be a real physical game. A lot of guys were banged up, coming off the field to get repaired and then going back in.

On the next-to-last play of the ball game, we were behind. John called on Lenny Moore to run a slant. Before John could get the ball off, Doug Atkins and a defensive tackle whose name I can't recall sacked John. They had somehow hit John in the face, and his nose was spurting blood all over the place.

John called timeout and went to the sideline to get his face cleaned up. Time for one more play. He came back into the huddle and called the exact same play. By this time, his nose had swelled so big, I don't know how he could see out of either eye. He hits Lenny Moore with the pass and Lenny scores the touchdown for us to win the ball game. It's incredible.

There were so many epic games with John. Just get him the ball when the game was still within reach, and he'd do it. Over and over again.

<hr>

TOM MATTE:

I can remember one game, the last game of the season, and it was Shula's first season as the coach. We were playing the Rams here in Baltimore.

The first half of the game, we took the tarp off of the field, and it was brutally cold. By the time the second half came around, we had to wear tennis shoes because there was ice out there. It was like an ice-skating rink.

That was the game in which we designed a play in which I would come out of the backfield and make my own move.

We were going down on the final drive, trailing the Rams, and John hit me with a pass going over the middle. I had come out of the backfield on a circle pattern, and I kept going across. The middle linebacker was coming over to get me, and I knew he wouldn't be able to stop because of the ice. I went right by him, caught the ball, bobbled it momentarily, and fell into the end zone, and we won the game.

That was one of the great games.

Another time we opened up the season, against whom I'm not sure—it might have been the Saint Louis Cardinals or even the Rams—but John popped me on a pass and I went eighty-eight yards for a touchdown. On another one I went for eighty yards on a lag draw, also for a touchdown. That was a great day.

FRANK "G-MAN" GITSCHIER, *who had left coaching to join the FBI as a special agent, remained close friends with Unitas long after their days together at Louisville. Gitschier kept close tabs on Unitas during and after his playing days:*

I remember once how a guy from ESPN was talking to John at a golf outing and brought up the subject of whether or not John got along with Shula. John said, "Well, no, we didn't get along that well at all. He was a young guy, and I had been in the league a long time and knew how to handle things."

Then the ESPN guy brought up the subject of the greatest game of all, the 1958 NFL Championship Game with the New York Giants. The guy said, "Bubba Smith once said there must have been something going on with the point spread in that game because you threw that pass right down by the goal line [instead of kicking a field goal]." And John said, "Bubba can't walk and chew game at the same time. There was nothing going on."

Coach Camp taught John how to call his own plays, and that's one thing that separated John from all the other quarterbacks. Now they have those headsets and lip readers. The reasons John and Shula didn't get along is that John insisted on calling his own plays, and that's the way it was going to be.

TOM MATTE, on being a friend of Unitas instead of just a teammate:

As far as having a relationship with John, there was a difference between him as a person and him as a player. As a player, he would be over on this side, and everyone else was over here. He had a couple of good friends who were players, such as Alex Hawkins and Bobby Boyd. I was a friend, but not in that little circle.

John liked Hawkins because he was funny, and he respected him because he got the most out of his ability. Hawkins was a smart player who communicated really well, and that connected with John. I also know that John respected me because he told me one time that I was the best back coming out of the backfield to catch passes that he had ever seen play the game.

In later life we became very good friends. We would play golf, I would see him at speaking engagements, doing this, doing that.

Because of an elbow injury, Unitas found himself embroiled in a bit of a quarterback controversy during the 1968 season. Late in training camp, coach **DON SHULA** *traded for New York Giants backup Earl Morrall. With Morrall filling in for Unitas, the Colts raced to a 13–1 season and then beat Minnesota and Cleveland for a berth in the 1969 Super Bowl game against Joe Namath and the New York Jets. By this time, Unitas felt he was healthy enough to resume starting, but Shula announced that he would be sticking with Morrall against the Jets, who would upset the Colts, 16–7. Shula:*

I may listen to the opinions of some players, but when a decision has to be made, I'm the one who makes it. I had no qualms about starting Morrall. He had a great year, leading us to fifteen victories, which was more than any quarterback had ever won. . . . During the course of the season, while we were winning with Earl and John was healing, Unitas was questioned time and time again about why he wasn't playing. His standard answer to reporters was cold: "Why don't you ask the Man?" That may have made it seem that we had a strange relationship. But that's not so. It's just John's way. . . .

As we approached Super Bowl time, John felt that he was now ready to go and that he deserved the chance to start because of his contributions to the Colts in previous years and previous championship games. He was disappointed when I told him that I was staying with Morrall. There was no reason to relegate Morrall to a reserve role.[5]

TOM MATTE:

I remember playing the Jets in a regular-season game after we had played them in the Super Bowl, and it turned into a duel between John and Joe Namath. Between them, they had something like nine hundred yards passing. It was a helluva game.

But John didn't get caught up in anything. He always had one focus out there—to win the football game. He couldn't care less about all the rest of the B.S. that goes on. He was a perfectionist at his position, and I believe he was the best quarterback who ever played.

***

ERNIE ACCORSI, *now general manager of the New York Giants, got his first job in the NFL as public relations director for the Colts in 1970, with Unitas's playing days in Baltimore winding down:*

By the time I got to the Colts, his legs were really bothering him. In the preseason of 1968, he had thrown a pass against the Dallas Cowboys, and he tore tendons in his elbow. They were little fibers that couldn't really be repaired. Some of them would regenerate, but not all of them.

Something was wrong, and they knew it. The year before, 1967, he had had a phenomenal year—he was throwing lasers. But after tearing the tendons in 1968, he couldn't throw for a while. That's why they went and got (Earl) Morrall. John got stronger later, but he never had the same velocity again.

Still, in the seventies he took us to the Super Bowl. In 1971, we had lost to Miami on the road, and then we were on the road in Oakland. The Raiders had an incredible record at their home stadium, but we couldn't afford to lose two games in a row if we wanted to make the playoffs. When John walked off the field in that game, we were ahead, 31–0, and we ended up winning, 37–14.

John threw the ball that day like he had always thrown it, and this was three years after the torn tendons had affected his throwing. I don't know what it was, but maybe the Good Lord said, "I'm going to give him one last day."

On the plane ride home John was almost giddy. He knew what he had experienced. It was almost like an epiphany. He had some pretty good games after that, but that was the last time I saw him throw like he had in his earlier years. It was like the Babe Ruth game in which he hit three home runs in Pittsburgh near the end of his career.

Unitas's last season with the Colts would be 1972, and it wasn't a fun time. Carroll Rosenbloom had sold the team to Robert Irsay. ACCORSI remembers:

The Rosenblooms didn't own the team anymore; Mr. Irsay did. A new general manager (Joe Thomas) came in in 1972, and he felt the team was getting old. He really didn't have any sensitivity to the heritage that John Unitas represented.

John was the guy who had taken football from the sand-lots to the number-one sport in America, just like Babe Ruth had done with baseball. Thomas fired the coach (Don McCafferty) and ordered the interim coach (John Sandusky) to play Marty Domres at quarterback. It was an unsettling season.

In the last game of the season, we lost to Miami, and that was the year the Dolphins had their perfect season. The Hall of Fame had called me and asked me to get everything John had worn that day and to send it to them. I went over to John's locker and told him about it, and he said, "You can have everything but my hightop shoes." I said, "Do I detect some sentimentality here?" And he said, "Hell, no. I love to wear them while cutting the grass. They help support my ankles."

It wasn't that Joe just got rid of Johnny—he sold him (to the San Diego Chargers), for $250,000. It was a sad day.

Thomas would make something like seventeen trades and give away most of the team, although he did rebuild the team and within two years won the division. But I'm talking about the feeling (or lack of it) he had for the authenticity of the franchise.

Granted, though, it was much more personal for me than from just being the P.R. director. Even when I had been the sports information director at Saint Joseph's College, I had had John's picture on my wall.

ACCORSI, *who was with the Colts from 1970 to 1975 and again from 1977 to 1983, reminisces:*

I was with John for his last three years with the Colts. I had grown up in Hershey, Pennsylvania, as a Baltimore Colts fan. This is where the Philadelphia Eagles trained, and they played the Colts every year in the first preseason game. I grew up with John Unitas, and by the time I got to the Colts, he was my idol.

The first time I met him, I was in my office the first or second day on the job. We had a bin of fan pictures that players used to grab and sign to be sent out. At one point I look up and he's just standing there. He looked over at me and said, "Hi, I'm Johnny Unitas." Like he really had to introduce himself. I somehow managed to babble out my name. It was the first year he had let his hair grow out, so it caught me off guard just a bit.

He was the most important player and the most important aspect of my job. He couldn't have been nicer to me, and over time we developed a friendship to the point where we spent Thanksgiving and Christmas Eves together. We were also members at the same country club in Baltimore, Hillendale. We had joined it because it was the first country club around that actually let Jews, Catholics, blacks, and everybody in.

When there was a country club slump going on and many were recruiting new members, one particular club came to me and asked if I would join. It was a restricted club, and when I asked them if they would have let my grandfather—who was Italian—in, they said no. So I wasn't going in, and then I called John and said, "They're now coming to see you." I knew what John was going to tell them—the same thing.

Former Colts teammate **ALEX HAWKINS** *was working for CBS-TV as a color man in 1972 when he was assigned to a game between the Colts and the Dallas Cowboys. Before the season, in a strange twist, Robert Irsay had bought the Rams and then traded them to Carroll Rosenbloom for the Colts. Baltimore was off to a 1–3 start with Unitas, now in his seventeenth season, still starting for the Colts. Hawkins:*

The Cowboys were in charge of the game, when suddenly and without warning, Johnny Unitas was benched. This was impossible, unheard of. For seventeen years this man had been performing last-minute miracles; it was unthinkable to jerk Unitas. To make matters worse, he was not benched by head coach Don McCafferty. He had been benched by Bob Irsay, the owner admittedly, but a man who had been around the game for only five weeks. A man with no previous experience in football or the National Football League.

Furthermore, John Unitas had been replaced by Marty Domres. I didn't even know who Domres was. I can't tell you how incensed I was. How could a man like Irsay with nothing more than money be allowed to do such a thing? Had the National Football League gone completely mad?[6]

4

JOHNNY U

One of the things that made John Unitas the classic American sports hero is that he didn't look like one, nor did he have the apparent pedigree. Yet he had a Horatio Alger-like life that was borderline rags to riches. Few people outside of family, friends, neighbors, and teammates had ever heard of him until he was well into his twenties and playing for the Baltimore Colts.

Among the many traits that Unitas had were an impeccable work ethic, courage, resiliency, and a strong arm. He could flat-out throw the football—maybe not through a wall, but almost exactly where it needed to be thrown to within a sixty-yard radius. Unitas invented the two-minute offense at least a decade before it was unveiled as a network-TV buzz phrase.

Authentic leaders come in all kinds of packages. Some appear almost brittle, a tad awkward, old school with buzz cuts, and laid-back with a low-key demeanor—just like John

Unitas. A measure of Unitas's greatness as a field general was his presence in a huddle: everyone else knew it was time to hush up, speak only when spoken to, and be prepared to be doused with another dose of confidence. Unitas had a knack for being creative and uncanny with his play calling, time and time again taking teams down the field for a score at a crucial moment in a big game. He did it over and over and over without all the shouting, pouting, or doubting.

Looks aren't everything.

Even in today's sophisticated game with computerized scouting tools and an eagle-eyed media that leaves no rock unturned, it's conceivable that a young Unitas wouldn't make it into the NFL. This time around, no one would draft him. He would be considered too scrawny, with slow feet, and lacking a major-college pedigree. Good arm? Get in line. Intangibles? Have a nice day, pal, and thanks for calling.

Let's be thankful the Baltimore Colts didn't overlook Johnny U.

SHIRLEY GREEN:

Didn't look like a star, until the game started.[1]

JOHN UNITAS, *on whether he had any regrets in life:*

I would have been a lot better student in high school than I was. But I had a very difficult time. My father died, and I had no one at home pushing me to open the books, or study, and that I regret to this day. I was able to get away with it then. Now you can't.[2]

SHIRLEY GREEN:

John had a commanding presence about him, being able to handle tough situations without getting anyone else around him upset. He would maintain that calm, and that's something he had as a kid.

CLARK WOOD, one of Unitas's Louisville coaches:

One of the reasons he got hurt as often as he did is that he would just hang in there and try to throw the ball, often waiting until the last second before he got hit. A lot of other quarterbacks would have gotten rid of it a lot sooner.

AP/WIDE WORLD PHOTOS

Johnny U, buzz cut and all, at the Westminister, Maryland, training camp in 1961.

WOOD contnues:

It took somebody terrific to go from Louisville to the pros. All John needed was that one chance, and he got that with the Colts. Once they saw him play in a game, they knew he was their man.

John loved football, and he was no-nonsense. Everything was positive about him—no minuses. I can't say that I knew going in that he would he would be one of the all-time great NFL quarterbacks, but I always believed he would be one of the top players.

Frank Otte, *a Louisville teammate, credits Unitas for keeping his ties to the university:*

John did a lot for the University of Louisville. He would continue to come back for some games long after he had left there, as well as for fund-raisers that went toward scholarships for students in the area.

Sometimes I and some other guys would see him at functions, and he was always getting on our case about not going up to see him in Baltimore. Here he was a major star, but he still wanted to be around his old friends and former college teammates.

Walter Fightmaster, *another Louisville colleague:*

As John became famous with the Colts, there was a tremendous desire on the parts of both the University of Louisville and the city of Louisville to acquire some notoriety for themselves from the fact that John had been developed here. Therefore, there was a tremendous desire to bring him back here on occasion. He was very willing to come back to Louisville to participate in fund-raisers, and with Frank Gitschier they would develop this Golden Arm Award. John did his best, regardless of all his other family and business involvement, to come back and help out at least once or twice a year. He was very good at that.

Louisville assistant coach **Joe Trabue:**

John's got to be one of the pillars of this program, even though he wasn't that famous when he was here.

I think the number-one reason for John being ranked the best quarterback ever was his leadership ability, his ability to control the huddle. Also, his ability to see the situation and call appropriate plays. His coaches were smart enough to turn him loose in that regard, contrary to what we do today. Then there was the tenacious attitude he had in working on things that could be perceived as weaknesses, say, a particular pass play.

Frank Gitschier, *who recruited Unitas to Louisville:*

John didn't care about statistics. You would say something about numbers to him, and he'd just shrug his shoulders and go, "Ahhhh, Coach."

Unitas wasn't exactly the kind of guy who would have people rolling in the aisles, but Louisville teammate **Michael McDonald** *claims Unitas wasn't all business all the time:*

He had a great sense of humor. If you got hurt and thought you might be too injured to play, he might look at you and say, "Well, you know you can spit on it. That'll work."

McDonald:

I never heard him say a curse word, either in a game or anywhere else.

UNITAS, *himself:*

A quarterback doesn't come into his own until he can tell the coach to go to hell.[3]

Legendary sportswriter **FRANK DEFORD,** *in a 2002* Sports Illustrated *tribute to Unitas following Unitas's death, reminisced about Unitas's arrival in Baltimore:*

Of course, no matter who John Constantine Unitas had played football for, it would've been Katie-bar-the-door. But perhaps never has greatness found such a fitting address. It wasn't only that Baltimore had such an inferiority complex, an awareness that all that stuck-up outlanders knew of our fair city was that we had crabs and white marble steps in profusion and a dandy red-light district, the Block. Since H. L. Mencken (he who had declared, "I hate all sports as rabidly as a person who likes sports hates common sense") had died, the most famous Baltimorean was a stripper, Blaze Starr. The city hadn't had a winner since the Old Orioles of a century past. For that matter, until very recently Baltimore hadn't even had a major league team in the 1900s. Before the Colts arrived in 1947, the best athlete in town was a woman duckpin bowler named Toots Barger. Football? The biggest games in Baltimore had been when Johns Hopkins took on Susquehanna or Franklin & Marshall at homecoming.[4]

Former player and network sports commentator **PAT SUMMERALL** *marveled at Unitas's play calling, and in talking about it refers to Tom Landry when Landry was the defensive coordinator for the New York Giants:*

He called his own plays, and he was totally unpredictable, which was what made him great. Coach Landry played defense based on percentages, but you couldn't do that with Unitas. He had the soul of a gambler. On third-and-one, you wouldn't get a running play.[5]

DON SHULA *was a Colts teammate with Unitas and would later become the team's head coach:*

I always felt that he invented the two-minute drill. He seemed to have a clock in his head and always knew how much time he had to work with. That skill was most evident in the NFL Championship Game in 1958.[6]

STEVE SABOL, *president of NFL Films, talks about how NFL Films segments of Unitas usually opened with a certain slow-motion establishing shot:*

We'd use a telephoto lens on the Colts breaking the huddle, and the shot would just be of his shoes, the black hightops approaching the line of scrimmage at Memorial Stadium, which never had any grass after the first two games of the season. It looked like a sandlot. And there wasn't a football fan in America who didn't know, from just that shot of the shoes, who it was and where it was. . . .

Because there were no domed stadiums, you could see the dust of Memorial Stadium, the frozen tundra of Lambeau, the vivid colors of Kezar Stadium. Cleveland Stadium was always wet—always. And we conveyed the passing of time. The games all started at one o'clock and ended in twilight, when Unitas was Rambo, coming down the field in the dust.[7]

TOM ARMSTRONG, *who played alongside Unitas at Louisville, wasn't surprised by Johnny U's eventual success, only that he had such a hard time getting the chance:*

John's success in the NFL with the Colts didn't really surprise me because I knew what his capabilities were. What surprised me was that he didn't get much of a chance right out of college. It seemed like no one really wanted him. He never talked about it much, though.

It can be kind of overwhelming to be associated with someone as famous as John, who only happens to be the greatest quarterback of all time. As I was moving up in the business world, I was always running into people who knew sports, whose first question out of their mouths after they heard I had played football at Louisville was if I knew and played with Unitas. Of course, nowadays, with younger people, a lot of them don't even know who Unitas is.

ALEX HAWKINS *gives an example of how Unitas could keep on playing while hurt, referring to a game against the Minnesota Vikings in the early sixties:*

I was still on the injured-reserve list, and standing behind the bench in street clothes, when Unitas came to the sideline with an injured finger on his throwing hand. There was absolutely no expression of pain on his face, just that deadpan look that he wore on game days. The middle finger on his right hand was dislocated in the shape of a Z.

(Trainer) Ed Block gently put it back in place. John just stood there like a man having his nails done: no grimace, no emotion, just that stone-cold stare. Then he trotted back to the huddle and threw a long pass on the next play. He had an incredible tolerance for pain. The year before, he had practiced and played with an ankle that was so swollen he could barely get his foot into those black hightop shoes.[8]

*There weren't many quarterbacks who could get the better of legendary linebacker **SAM HUFF**, but he always figured Unitas had just about everyone's number:*

Unitas did the same thing all the time, he just did it better than anybody else. He had me so psyched in playing defense against him, I thought he could read my mind. He always seem to know what I was going to do. On third and one, he might throw the ball to Berry or Mutscheller or Moore. On running downs, he would often throw the ball, and on passing downs, he'd sometimes run the ball. We couldn't get a book on him. He studied defenses and had a knack for knowing what to do in all kinds of situations.

One time, when I was playing for the Washington Redskins, I called nine different defenses, and he beat me every time. Finally, I got into the huddle and asked if anybody had a suggestion, if there was a defense they wanted to call. Nobody said a word.

Unitas was a dominating quarterback, and he never changed expressions. On one play during that '58 game in New York, he had the ball and I hit him with everything I had, and I thought I had sacked him. Yeah, I had him down, only to find out that he had gotten the ball off over my head and completed the pass to Raymond Berry. I mean, I body-slammed him—he was tough! And he never complained, no matter how hard some guys hit him.

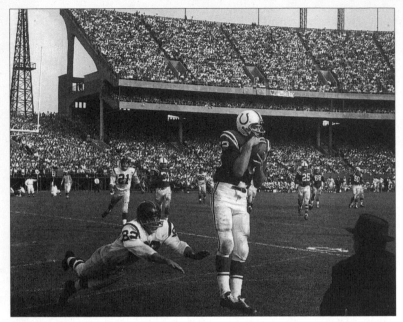

A scene that took place dozens of times over the years: Raymond Berry catching a TD pass from Unitas.

HUFF weighs in with an assessment of the great quarterbacks of his era:

Unitas was the most consistent quarterback I ever played against. In fact, if he wasn't the greatest I played against, I don't know who in the hell was. I think Sonny (Jurgenson) was a terrific quarterback, but he didn't have the team that Unitas had. Johnny had a great offensive line and defense, and they were solid all around—just like the Giants in those days.

I still cannot imagine the Pittsburgh Steelers cutting John Unitas. Holy cow! I don't know whose decision it was to cut him, but that guy's desk deserved to get cleaned out long ago. John Unitas came from nowhere, just like a guy who played and starred for the New York Giants, Emlen Tunnell—he came from nowhere.

Every time we played against the Colts, my wife—we're now divorced—would tell me before the game, "Don't you hit John." I said, "What?" "You can hit anybody else you want, but I don't want to see you hit John Unitas." She thought the world of John Unitas, but I made it clear to her that I was going to hit him every chance I got.

I'm not saying John was a great-looking guy, but women liked him because he had a mystique about him. I'm not saying I was better looking than John, but my nose was—it didn't get broken as many times as his did. John looked a little bit like Clint Eastwood—he could have played a western part in the movies or on TV. He might have looked at me, squinted, and said, "Go ahead, Sam, I'm going to make your day."

He was great to play against, even though he took the fun out of the game. We beat him once, in Baltimore, in the opening game of the season. I intercepted a pass in the game.

LENNY LYLES, *a Unitas teammate at Louisville and later with the Colts:*

Unitas performed so well all the time, it's hard to pick out just one game that you could label the most memorable. He did whatever it took to win, and he knew how to win. That might have made it a little tough for his coaches, because John was a take-charge guy. He knew what would work and what wouldn't work, and he knew what he could do and what he couldn't do. If I were putting a football team together, I would start with John Unitas at quarterback and Jim Brown at running back.

RAYMOND BERRY, *on his kinship with Unitas:*

We had a lot of things in common, and it started with the fact that we both took our football very seriously. We were working hard all the time to get better, and neither one of us tolerated screwing up. I didn't like to drop a pass, and he didn't like to miss one. Neither one of us wanted to be half-ass about anything.

Also, we were both mentally tough. In college, I had been primarily a defensive player, and I loved playing defense. When I came to professional football, I had to switch over, but that defensive mentality never left me. Matter of fact, John Unitas would have made a great middle linebacker. He was the type of guy who liked to get after people, and he could knock you on your butt if he wanted to.

We had a common bond in wanting to do extra work, which just didn't happen very much. It's rare to have players willing to do the "extra extra." Unitas and I were both that way. Our work ethic would be extremely significant to our being able to work together so well over so many years. We just did it naturally without thinking about it a whole lot. It allowed us to do things as a quarterback-receiver combination that went beyond the norm.

Most of what we did together for extra work was during training camp and the season. It's not like we hung out for a couple hours each day in the off-season working on throws, timing, and pass patterns. After the season ended in December, all the players scattered to the four winds, and there were no off-season gatherings like they have now with all the minicamps and so forth.

The way practices were structured in those days, we were allowed to spend as much time after practice out on the field putting in extra work. What you run into today is that things are so highly organized that when on-field practice is over, then you go straight to the weight room or the film room for a whole bunch of other scheduled stuff.

All it takes is ten or fifteen minutes after practice with you and the quarterback, just the two of you, you could get a lot of stuff done, such as getting the timing of the patterns down. Or just talk football. And if you wanted to repeat a move over and over without a bunch of other distractions around, you could do it. You can get more done one-on-one with a quarterback during those ten or fifteen minutes than you can in a whole two-hour practice.

As much as **BERRY** *marveled at Unitas's seemingly limitless work ethic, Johnny U did have his limits:*

Every once in a while John would get a little testy about something. One time I came to him with my list of things to go over, and he wasn't in the mood to talk football. So he kind of brushed me off. But I tried not to be oversensitive because I was back the next day.

In working individually with John Unitas, and this was something that in training camp happened over and over, for us to start hitting on the long ball, it took a heck of a lot of work.

I remember working with John after practice on the long ones. He would throw it too far outside, too far inside, underthrow it, overthrow it—we just kept working on it, and after a while I could feel him starting to get the range.

Of all the long balls John threw to me in games over the years, I'll bet he didn't really miss on more than one or two. I remember one game against the Packers in which we faked the quick post and went deep and broke it wide open, and it was an overthrow of about two yards. Other than that, I don't remember him missing one like that.

FRANK GITSCHIER:

John's record of forty-seven consecutive games with at least one touchdown pass will never be broken. I read a sports study somewhere that listed it as the second-greatest sports accomplishment by one person in history, behind only the one hundred points that Wilt Chamberlain scored in a basketball game in 1962. John's record was even ranked ahead of Joe DiMaggio's hitting streak of fifty-six games.

GITSCHIER tells of the time his association with Johnny U got him an audience with the legendary New York writer Jimmy Breslin:

Sometime after Johnny had been voted the greatest player to play in the greatest game, the 1958 NFL Championship Game, I was in the New York office of the FBI when writer Jimmy Breslin called me. He told me he wanted to interview me for a story he was doing on Johnny Unitas. He had been to Louisville to interview some people down there, and they had told him he needed to talk to me.

I asked my agent in charge for permission to do the interview, and he said I could, because it was about something that had been a part of my life before I joined the FBI. The only stipulation was that this had better not be an FBI endorsement of Johnny Unitas.

I took four hours of annual leave to avoid any suggestion of a conflict of interest, and I met Jimmy down at a bar near Penn Station. He tried to get me to say that I was responsible for Johnny's success. I told him, "Coach [Frank] Camp is the guy responsible for his success, and all I did was teach him the basic fundamentals of how to play quarterback."

Well, the big article came out in *Collier's* magazine—
"The Quarterback Nobody Wanted." I got about two lines in
there. That was after we had spent all that time together,
although we drank beer and had a good time, and I did get
to take the train home early that night. I wasn't upset a bit
about the short mention given me, because I knew from
reading the article that a lot of the background had come
from me. So I knew it had been time well spent.

The only time I have been a role player in my whole life
was when it came to John Unitas, and I was filling my role.
My loyalty has always been to John, and I always tried to
stay in the background when the pictures were being taken.

ALEX HAWKINS:

He had the highest pain tolerance of any man I've ever
known. He wouldn't even take aspirin because, he said, "It
makes me goofy." He did all that without any kind of
painkiller, as far as I know.

TOM MATTE *elaborates on Unitas's command of the huddle:*

John would always come back to the huddle, and he was the
voice—nobody talked. He had total control, but every once
in a while, when we got back to the huddle, he might look at
me and say, "Matte, what do you have?" Or he would also
ask the same question of Jimmy Orr, Lenny Moore, John
Mackey, or Raymond Berry: "What do you have?," or "What
are you setting up?"

Jimmy Orr might say, "Hey, I need about five or six more
plays because I'm setting up the corner pattern, and I'll be

ready in about five plays." With Raymond, he would say, "What kind of move do you have, something to the inside or to the outside?" And Berry would say, "I have the outside move," or "A max pattern over the middle."

When you came back and said you had something, you had better be right. He would go to you in a critical situation and say, "Okay, I need you *right* now. What do you have going?" And you spoke only when you were spoken to.

That's the input players had back then, where today the coaches know more than the players do—or at least they think they do. They don't.

MATTE gets downright wistful when talking about his Colts:

There will never again be a team like there was in Baltimore. I have talked this over with Ernie Accorsi, who's now with the New York Giants but was the Colts P.R. guy for a number of years. We have asked each other, "Will there ever again be a relationship between a team, a city, and a state like there was with Baltimore?"

This town lived and died with us. I never had a season ticket when I played for the Colts because we were always sold out. Every game. When my parents came to see a game, they had to sit in the bleachers. We were allowed to have two free tickets, which I let my wife use, and she would sit with all the other wives in a corner of an end zone.

The people of Baltimore knew our birthdays; they knew our wives' and children's names; they knew where we worked in the off-season; and we had listed telephone numbers. The fans would send us birthday cards. It was a respect between the players and the fans. There were Colt Corrals all over town, and we would go out as players and visit them.

We had a basketball team that went around raising money for charity. John and I played guard on the team, and John was a terrific player. We had a helluva basketball team. We'd pick up fifty dollars a game each, and that was our beer money. After the game we might go out and have a few beers, fans included.

HAROLD ROSENTHAL, *writer and author, on Unitas's streak of forty-seven consecutive games with one or more TD passes:*

It extended from the first week of December 1956 through the middle of December 1960. Equally as amazing was the fact that it was not in the books for a long time, at least not the details. Colts writers talked about Unitas's streak, but no one had chapter and verse. It had to be dug out of the old score sheets, this in contrast with Joe DiMaggio's fifty-six-game hitting streak in '41, when there were several dozen chroniclers on the job delineating every ball and strike.

Unitas threw six dozen TD passes in that forty-seven-game sequence. He had three receivers who caught TD passes from him in double figures: Jim Mutscheller, twenty-three; Raymond Berry, twenty-three; and Lenny Moore, seventeen. All principals, except Mutscheller, are in the Hall of Fame, along with other Colts of that era: Jim Parker, Artie Donovan, Gino Marchetti, and, of course, the coach, Weeb Ewbank.

There were seven games in which Unitas threw four TDs, and an oddity was that the streak started with a loss at Los Angeles and finished with a loss at Los Angeles. Green Bay presented him with a punctured lung that kept him out of a couple of games (they don't count in a streak; it's only when you play), and he played several games with a flak jacket someone fashioned out of a few old washboards.[9]

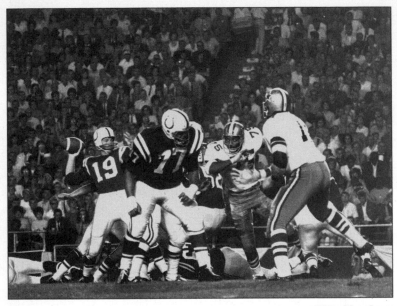

Unitas, sometime in the 1960s, looks to throw against Dallas as the Cowboys' Jethro Pugh attacks the middle trying to find a way to stop Johnny U.

Sportswriter **TOM CALLAHAN** *was a young reporter covering high schools for the* Baltimore Evening Sun *when he was assigned to write a sidebar after a Colts game. Admittedly timid when he got to the locker room, a shy Callahan was greeted by Raymond Berry, who answered some questions and then asked if the scribe wanted to speak to anyone else. Callahan:*

"Well, yes, I guess Unitas." So Berry yells, "Hey, John, come here a minute!" And Unitas leaves an interview in front of his locker and comes over, and Berry says, "John, say hello to my friend Tom Callahan of the *Evening Sun*." Unitas pulls up a stool and starts calling me "Tommy." "Well,

Tommy, here's what we did. We wanted to do this, so we worked such and such a play." And he goes on at length. We just sat there and talked. I remember a TV guy approaching sort of gingerly, and Unitas giving him kind of a dirty look. Finally, I had everything, and he says, "Need anything else, Tommy?"[10]

UNITAS, *on the fame his football exploits generated:*

Those kinds of things never fazed me. The notoriety and the celebrity and all that kind of stuff. I just go my way and do what I think is right, and if people like it fine, and if they don't it's not my problem.[11]

Writer **LARRY L. KING** *offered this nutshell assessment of Unitas in a 1968 magazine article:*

On some teams a Super Star is only minimally approachable to ordinary ballplayers and not at all to rookies; such men are deferred to as royally as they demand to be. One learns, however, that Super Star Unitas comes on pure Boy Scout. He regularly brings in cases of Nehi Red, a soft drink he picks up at cut-rate prices somewhere, to a young and relatively obscure Colt who thirsts after them. When Notre Dame's Terry Hanratty, then a callow junior, wrote his idol asking how to avoid the horrors of pass interceptions, he promptly received a helpful essay on how to spot secondary receivers and the importance of standing firm and cool under fire ("Learn to eat the ball or scramble when a receiver is in trouble."). Unitas never hazes rookies; he drinks only beer, and that in moderation; he smokes not at all; and if there is any of the philanderer in him it is well concealed. He is a sucker for kids, rarely able to resist their pleas for autographs, pictures, helmet chin straps, an occasional football. He takes pains to quietly thank and encourage those ditch-digging linemen whose work wins football games but rarely lands them in the headlines.[12]

UNITAS, *on fans:*

You're a hero when you win and a bum when you lose. That's the game. They pay their money, and they can boo if they feel like it.[13]

Rams defensive tackle **MERLIN OLSEN** *was long a part of the fabled Fearsome Foursome, although Unitas never was one to buy into the fearsome part:*

He waits until the last possible second to release the ball, even if it means he's going to take a good lick. When he sees us coming, he knows it's going to hurt and we know it's going to hurt, but he just stands there and takes it. No other quarterback has such class.

I swear that when he sees you coming out of the corner of his eye, he holds that ball a split second longer than he really needs to—just to let you know he isn't afraid of any man. Then he throws it on the button. I weigh 270, myself, and I don't know if I could absorb the punishment he takes. I wonder if I could stand there, week after week, and say, "Here I am. Take your best shot."[14]

PAUL ZIMMERMAN, *longtime senior football writer for* **Sports Illustrated:**

Physically he had it all—the whiplike delivery, the athletic ability, the great sense of timing and, oh, man, the courage. He had to do it the hard way. The NFL hadn't liberalized the passing rules. His receivers could get mugged downfield. Defensive linemen could head-slap their way into the back-field, and when they homed in on a quarterback they could hit him any way they wanted. None of today's cellophane-wrapper protection from the officials.

And Unitas got it plenty. He'd snarl and wipe the blood off his face and lead his team down the field on another of his great scoring drives, operating in that hunch-shouldered way of his, with the herky-jerky setup and deadly accuracy. Eighteen years of that.[15]

BILL CURRY recalls how Unitas provided an inspirational example one day when Curry was struggling to make the Colts during a sweltering training camp in 1967:

I didn't know if I was going to make the team. It was 106 degrees that morning, and John came onto the field whistling. I said, "Why are you whistling?" He said, 'You know, Billy, you're a long time dead. So you better enjoy every day. I love football practice." I knew I had been chal-lenged. I had no choice but to respond. That's what great leaders do. He was just trying to help the terrified new guy find his place. We had a newborn daughter, and I didn't know how I'd provide for her.[16]

ALEX HAWKINS:

John Unitas was *the* quarterback. No one ever knew or cared what John's salary called for. On his arm rested the hopes of the team. The one cardinal rule on the team was to keep Unitas healthy. To allow John to be hit was a sure one-way ticket home. Without John and his leadership the season was over. It is impossible to exaggerate the blind, unquestioning faith this team had in that man. Greatness can sometimes be measured more accurately not by what one man can do, but rather by what one man can inspire others to do. When John was on the field anything was possible. The Colts didn't just think that; they knew it.[17]

Not everything that Unitas did inspired faith in him.
HAWKINS:

Driving down that expressway toward Washington reminded me of Johnny Unitas. I always rode with him to the airport for our road games. He drove eighty miles an hour, right on the bumper of another car. It scared me to death, and when I asked him what he would do if the other car hit the brakes, he would always say, "Got no reason to brake—the road goes all the way to Washington."[18]

*As best as **SAM HUFF** can remember, if Unitas ever spoke to an opposing player, it certainly wasn't to him:*

On the field, Unitas was all business. He didn't speak to opposing players. Lots of players trash talk today, but back then we felt like we needed to concentrate so much on what we were doing that we felt we couldn't afford to be doing a whole lot of talking. I might say something to an offensive lineman for holding me or something like that, but otherwise I was so busy calling out defenses and shifts that you just didn't have time to trash talk.

As well and as long as **RAYMOND BERRY** *knew Unitas, there really wasn't much in the way of deep conversation between the two:*

It was usually me who would initiate the discussions and work sessions that Johnny and I had. I would come with a list and then we would go over it, one thing at a time.

Most of the time there really wasn't a whole lot to talk about. What we would do is get out on the field and work on things. I remember rehearsing a scramble situation, where I would start running a pass pattern and then turn around and see him trying to get out of the pocket.

We would also work on routes. Once I got more experienced, I started getting very precise about those routes and developing multiple fakes. I might have one basic pattern with six or seven different ways of running it, and John and I would rehearse all those things. And it got to where Johnny could read every one of my body movements, like how I was going to plant my shoulder and everything else.

I got to know him pretty well. A guy easy to approach and to talk to, a guy with a good sense of humor. At the same time, he wasn't an easy guy to really get to know.

He had strong convictions. For one thing, he had no patience with guys who wouldn't work. Of course, I don't either. If you really understand the opportunity you have in professional football, you know it's going to last only a short time. If you haven't got sense enough to take advantage of it to the fullest, then you just don't have a brain that works. It's so difficult even to just get a chance, and to not give it 100 percent probably drove John Unitas crazier than anything else could.

BERRY *gives his thoughts on rating the great quarter-backs of all time:*

Because I also spent twenty-five years in coaching, my perspective on judging talent has changed a lot. As a coach, you just give me one out of any of the twenty or twenty-five greatest quarterbacks you would name, and I would be happy. Any one of them, and I know I could darn well win with them, from Norm Van Brocklin, Johnny Unitas, and Sonny Jurgenson to Roger Staubach and Terry Bradshaw. There's just been so many great quarterbacks.

You can't judge a quarterback totally by the number of championships won because the quarterback is so dependent on having the good fortune to be with a team that got its act together. That goes back to the ownership of the team, because that sets the tone of who and what the coach is. There have been some very good quarterbacks who have been stuck their whole careers, or most of their careers, with a poorly run and poorly owned team. Archie Manning, for example. Dan Marino, for that matter, never played with a *complete* team.

John and I were at the right place at the right time with the right people, and that has so much to do with how a quarterback is perceived, and he doesn't have any doggone control over it. I see what Joe Montana and Jerry Rice had with the Forty-niners as a replica of what John and I fell into with the Colts. Bill Walsh knew what he was doing, and that is crucial.

I didn't have close to the abilities of some of the receivers I have since seen over the years, and I'm speaking straight as a personnel guy. Baltimore was the perfect place for me, because it was a place where players were given wide latitude in which to operate. That's unusual, and we had an unusual quarterback in John Unitas, and that played to my strengths.

*Former quarterback **JOE THEISMANN** came into the
NFL just as Unitas's career was winding down:*

Watching Unitas was like watching Arnold Palmer swing a
golf club. Nobody has a swing like Arnold, and no one
dropped back and delivered the football like Unitas. He was
distinctive, efficient, and great at what he did.

    In later years, I had an opportunity to get to know John.
At first, it was tough to say anything to him. Out of respect
and awe, I sort of sat there with a stupid stare on my face.
But I saw him at autograph sessions and went out to dinner
with him, and I used to love to listen to the stories.[19]

*__FRANK GITSCHIER__, himself a former quarterback at
Louisville, spent many spare moments at that university
tutoring the young Unitas in the finer points of quarterbacking:*

In those days we coaches would work all summer with
players, like we did with John. One year, while some of us
coaches were going to school in Nashville during the summer, I had classes only four days a week, so I would come
back to Louisville on Thursday night and work with john
on Friday, Saturday, and Sunday. Then at 4:00 A.M. on
Monday we'd head back down to Nashville. John was just
an excellent guy to coach, and he was smart—he remembered everything.

    One year I went to Baltimore when he was living in either
Towson or Lutherville. He took me down to his basement
and I saw where he had these wooden cabinets all around the
room. He opened them up and showed me all these trophies
and awards he had stuffed in there. Some of the more

prestigious awards, like his Jim Thorpe Award, he had out on display upstairs in what he called his recreation room.

He took me up there, and that's where I saw this stack of film sitting right next to this machine. He would just sit there and break it all down—it was film of opposing teams, and he would chart what each player on that defense did. He did his homework. It was the same way at Louisville, and we had it where the quarterback had to learn everybody's position on the field as well as everybody's plays. That's because you might call a play in the huddle that they hadn't seen in a couple of weeks, and the quarterback would have to be able to remind any of the other ten guys exactly what they were supposed to do on that play.

For a number of years after he left coaching to join the FBI, GITSCHIER worked in New York, certainly close enough to go see some of his buddy's games:

One time the Colts came to play in Yankee Stadium in the late sixties, and John was out with an injury. Earl Morrall was playing for him. They beat the Giants pretty decisively.

But John had told me before the game to bring my kids to the locker room. So I take Frank Jr. and Greg, and we go down there. They would always close the locker room door at first, after the game, to give them time to pray and for the coach to talk to them. Then they would open up the doors to the media.

You know how the New York media is, just packing in. The kids and I were standing way in back, with what must have been twenty-five guys in front of us, blocking our view. John Sandusky, who was in charge of the locker room, came out and he yells out, "Are you Johnny Unitas's coaching friend? You can come in first." So it was like the

AP/Wide World Photos

In this 1966 game against the Minnesota Vikings, Unitas passed for four touchdowns to pass Y. A. Tittle as the NFL's career leader in TD throws, with 214.

parting of the waves, and we walked right in. That was really something.

ALEX HAWKINS, *giving another tribute to the value of John Unitas:*

I think he was the greatest quarterback. What he did for the game is like wondering, *Who's the greatest golfer?* In my mind it's Arnold Palmer because of what he has done for the game.

People forget that back when John started playing, not everybody was selling out their stadiums. But the Colts were selling out Memorial Stadium, chiefly because of Johnny Unitas. We sold out a lot of our road games. John *was* the game of professional football, and he did what Palmer did for golf.

TOM MATTE:

He got better as the years went on because he got more knowledgeable. But he had some injuries that really set him back.

He had a nickname, "Zip," because he could zip the ball so fast. But in '68, he tore off a muscle inside his right elbow, something he didn't fully figure out until years later, and that's why later in life he couldn't pinch his fingers together.

John knew how to throw the fastball, how to lay it out for you to run under, how to throw it away from the defensive backs—low and to the outside. He always had the right pass at the right time, and that's why I think he was the most complete passer of all time. A lot of these guys have the arm to really zing out, like Bert Jones, who could put it through the wall, but why do that when you have a guy wide open? Let him run under it and catch it with his soft hands.

One of Unitas's best friends over the last twenty-five years of his life was Baltimore-area auto dealer **RICHARD SAMMIS:**

John was not the most agile quarterback in the world, but he made it all up by being smart. He was so good at reading defenses; he knew if the linebacker he was keying on was in view over the middle, that there would be a receiver open out to one of the sides.

He learned the easiest routes—don't make it any harder on yourself. If you know what the defense is going to do, go to the place you have a better chance of running or throwing the ball.

ERNIE ACCORSI, *former P.R. director for the Colts, remembers another classic Unitas moment that occurred late in his career:*

There was a play that he made against Houston with the clock running down. He threw a post-corner to Roy Jefferson for a touchdown. I couldn't believe my own eyes— I saw John turn and walk to the bench right after he threw the ball and before Roy had even caught it. It won the game, and John never even saw the end of the play.

On the plane ride back, I asked, "Did you see Jefferson catch that ball?"

"No."

"How could you do that?"

"Because I knew I had thrown it perfectly, and there was nothing else I could do."

After a loss—it was gone. John had amnesia about the loss. He never dwelled on it. He could categorize it, and that was the end of it. It was next week.

You'd say to him, "Don't you feel the pressure?" And he'd say, "I have a job to do." There was nothing phony about it.

ACCORSI *continues:*

One time in 1972 I was sitting in his restaurant (the Golden Arm) and I asked him to take me through the (overtime) drive against the Giants (in the 1958 NFL Championship Game). He recounted every play to me by name. This was fourteen years after the fact.

In 1978, they had a twenty-year anniversary touch football game in Central Park between players from those two teams. It was like five against five. I knew the Giants guys included Charlie Conerly, Kyle Rote, and Rosey Grier; and we had Johnny, Lenny (Moore), (Raymond) Berry, and (Alan) Ameche. It wasn't anything formal, and CBS filmed it as kind of a party-type thing.

Lenny said John was calling plays in the huddle, by name, just like he had twenty years earlier. Lenny said to John, "You really want to win this, don't you?" And Johnny said, "Well, that's what we're here for." That was John.

ACCORSI:

Both physically and mentally, John's the toughest human being I've ever been around, and I've been around a lot of tough people in my life.

He had a lot of physical problems later in life, and that's because he got beat up so much during his playing career. I've always thought it takes five times more courage to stay in the pocket than to run out of it. You can control your own destiny when you're scrambling and running. He would hold the ball until the last second.

Dick Lynch, who had been a defensive cornerback for us and is now a broadcaster, tells the story of how he came on a corner blitz: "And he looked right at me and he knew I was going to hit him hard. No one was blocking me and John knew I was going to level him. He had a good two or three seconds to get rid of the ball or brace himself. But he held it until the fraction of a second before I nailed him, and I just hit him with everything I had. When I got up to look, there was Berry downfield running with the ball."

RICHARD SAMMIS:

John had four championship rings and he never wore any of them. They might have meant something to him personally, but he didn't feel a need to be showing them off.

John didn't believe in collections. His hobby was spending time with his family.

SAMMIS proffers more insight on his love for the Colts and his association with Unitas:

My relationship with John dates back about twenty-five years. I met him through football. I was a big fan and a sponsor of the Colts. It started with a radio show that we sponsored on Monday nights at the Golden Arm. John and another gentleman, Bob Bartel, did the radio show. That's how I got involved with the team and with John as a friend. We became very good friends through that. In fact, his office was right down the hall from mine.

I have lived in the Baltimore area my whole life. I was a big Colts fans, absolutely. John was always the man. He was the Baltimore Colts, which is not to diminish Artie Donovan, Gino Marchetti, or any of the other stars. John represented the NFL in Baltimore. All the other players did their part, but John was special.

The greatest quote ever made about Johnny Unitas was made by Jon Faccenda, the gentleman who had the great voice and did all those voice-overs for NFL Films. There's a tape out called "The Best Ever." They compare all the great quarterbacks. It gets right down to the very end, and all of a sudden they play this grandiose music and the smoke clears, and there's John. At this point, Faccenda says, "Many have been compared to John Unitas, but John Unitas has been compared to no one." That quote has stayed with me my whole life. Not only was that true in football, but it was also true in his personal life. He was the best. *The best.*

HAROLD ROSENTHAL *discusses what it was like to work with Unitas on the book* Playing Pro Football to Win. *Rosenthal said that the working relationship was for him to write a chapter or two, then send it to Unitas at his home in Lutherville, Maryland, for approval:*

The stuff from Unitas seemed to be coming back in record time. Mailed one day, back two days later. Maybe he wasn't even looking at the stuff, perish the thought. So a little trick was resorted to. The pages were sent him, one or two out of order. Back they came, still out of order. Marvelous.

Now the book was published, and a great many mutual friends rallied to give it a push via favorable publicity. In Baltimore the veteran Colts beat man for the Sun . . . Cameron Snyder, asked John by way of openers, "See you wrote a new book?"

"Yup," answered the greatest quarterback in the history of the NFL, voted thusly at the fiftieth anniversary celebration of the league.

"How is it?" asked Cam, figuring he'd get the conversation started.

"Don't know," replied John. "Haven't read it yet."[20]

Unitas joins his good pal Richard Sammis for food and fellowship during a trip to Florida.

Receiver **ED HINTON** *caught the last touchdown pass thrown by Unitas as a Baltimore Colt. Hinton recalls one game in 1970 in which Unitas rallied the Colts from a 17–0 deficit to beat the Chicago Bears, 21–20, despite two dropped balls by Hinton on the second of those three touchdown drives:*

John was always Mr. Unitas to me. In that drive, John threw a perfect pass, and I dropped it between my legs. He called the same play, a fifteen-yard curl, and I dropped another perfect pass. On fourth down, he waves off the field-goal unit. He calls my number, and I made a one-handed catch on the sideline for a first down at the Bears' seven. We score, and I am emotionally distraught. I said, "Mr. Unitas, why did you go to me a third time?" He said, "Because I knew you were going to catch the damned ball."[12]

Veteran football writer **PAUL ZIMMERMAN** *has called Unitas the consummate NFL quarterback, the greatest who ever lived:*

Some of the most successful long passes have been deliberate underthrows. Unitas and (Joe) Namath both perfected it. A receiver goes deep, turns and comes back for the ball, at which point the defender gets his feet crossed and falls down, and the offense is six points richer. In the press box we're saying, "What luck!" but often it's planned.[22]

JOHN UNITAS, *on how he spent his last season, 1973, with the San Diego Chargers working with a rookie quarterback by the name of Dan Fouts, as told to* Sports Illustrated's *Paul Zimmerman:*

The coach, Harland Svare, asked me to work with Danny, and Dan was all excited about it. Then after five or six games, the offensive coach, Bob Schnelker, came over to me and said, "The coaches had a meeting last night, and we'd rather you didn't work with him anymore." Who knows why? Anyway, I told Fouts, and oh, boy, he was hot. So I said, "What the hell, we'll keep doing it. They're not smart enough to know what's going on anyway."[23]

CHRIS REDMAN, *a Baltimore Ravens quarterback who won the Johnny Unitas Golden Arm Award while playing at the University of Louisville, saw Unitas as his hero:*

He was the definition of old school. When you think about tough, hard-nosed players who played with broken hands, he was the person I would think of. The more I watched him, the more I wanted to be like him. Then I learned about the things he did off the field. He signed autographs and tried to get to know the people he signed for. That's just something special.[24]

Part of John Unitas's legacy will always be two statues of him, one at the University of Louisville and the other outside Ravens Stadium in Baltimore. **FRANK GITSCHIER:**

John didn't express himself overtly, but he was impressed when they unveiled the statue here at Louisville.

One of the main characteristics as to how you treated Johnny was not to promote him. When I went to him to start the Unitas Golden Arm Award, he wasn't too keen on that because it would have been us promoting him. He said, "What you see with me is what you get, that's it." I told him, "Well, you and Butkus went into the Hall of Fame close to each other, and they now have a Butkus Award, and they're doing something for charity. We'll go with scholarship awards as part of this and give scholarships to kids coming out of high school." So, reluctantly, he let me go ahead and do it.

We were members of the Kentucky chapter of the National Football Foundation's College Football Hall of Fame. I went to them and said I want to do this, and rather reluctantly they allowed me to start this award. We were the only chapter now that had a national award associated with it. Of course, it was John Unitas.

After about seven or eight years of doing this with the foundation, we felt we were doing a lot of work without a lot of support, and we weren't generating enough money to be able to do all the things that we wanted to do. So we started our own foundation. We also decided that neither John nor I would have anything to do with the selection process, to include the selection of the candidates or any of the voting. We average between twelve and fourteen members every year who do the selection and the voting.

We award about $30,000 every year to local kids. They are selected by their own schools based on citizenship, academics, athletics, leadership, and community participation. They exemplify what Johnny Unitas exemplified on the field. Each of those kids get a thousand dollars to start their college education. These are the Scholar-Athlete Awards, and they were brought down to have their picture taken with John. Then they have their pictures taken with the winner of the Golden Arm Award, who this year (2002) happened to be Carson Palmer, who also won the Heisman Trophy the next day. It's a nice deal all around.

GITSCHIER *offers some more explanation on how the Golden Arm voting works:*

The criteria for the award is that each candidate must be completing his college eligibility that year. No further eligibility. One year we had a tie, and we had nothing set up for a tiebreaker. I went to John and told him this. He said, "What the hell are we going to do?" Then he said, "Who didn't vote for one of the two guys that tied?" I told him who it was, and John said, "Well, let's call him up and make him choose between the two." He did, and we had a winner.

Sometime after John Unitas passed away, his former Colts teammate **TOM MATTE** *gathered together* *some ex-quarterbacks for a roundtable discussion and videotaped them talking about the game. Matte:*

We had a roundtable about the game and the influence John had on the game. We videotaped it, and we're going to produce it and sell it and market it. I had Joe Kapp, Sonny Jurgenson, Roman Gabriel, Billy Kilmer, Earl Morrall, and myself.

We sat around and talked for a long time about the role of quarterbacks now versus the role of quarterbacks back then. With the way they play now, they are pretty much just muppeteers, almost like cyborgs, programmed by coaches. When we played, the coaches would come in with a game plan on Tuesday, we'd take it home to review it and to study film, and then we'd come back and give our feedback and input, to include changing some things around.

John would look at the film and say, "Here's what I can do against this defense here and against this defense there." The receivers would have their say, and then it was all assimilated together. That became the real game plan. It worked out very well. I think Brian Billick with the (Baltimore) Ravens lets his players have some input, which is a smart thing to do. Some of these other guys have egos too big to let others have input—they want to do the whole thing so they can get credit for it.

You don't win with coaches. You win with players who execute and know how to take advantage of things and make it happen. Today's games are *productions* instead of *games*. It's almost like games are choreographed to some extent, whereas our games were more authentic, down and dirty and mud and all that stuff, and nobody was doing all the high-fives and all the rest of that B.S. that goes with it.

One thing that really upsets me, and it used to upset Johnny, too, is when some team is losing a game, 21–0, but one of their guys sacks the opposing quarterback, and he comes out of it dancing. What are you celebrating? I mean, you're behind, 21–0. Why would you even say anything, let alone dance around? Stuff like that used to drive Johnny nuts.

If I had spiked the ball into the end zone as a player, there would have been three guys fighting to get to me first to stick the ball up my butt: John Unitas, Gino Marchetti, or Artie Donovan. You just didn't do that kind of stuff. It's a different game. The guy bringing a pen out of his sock to sign an autograph on a football? I'd have taken that pen and stuck it in his ear. Everyone's looking for a gimmick now.

***FRANK GITSCHIER** never played a down in the NFL, yet he was the go-to guy when Unitas found out in 1979 that he was going to be enshrined in the Pro Football Hall of Fame and needed to designate a presenter to introduce him. Gitschier explains:*

I had retired from the FBI in 1978. I worked the bank-robbery squad in New York for the FBI in the late sixties and early seventies. Jack Dennehy was the Mafia supervisor of the FBI in New York at the time. Jack went on to become director of security for the National Football League, and his son and Frank, our oldest boy, had played high school ball together.

I called Jack one day in January 1979 and asked him if he had heard anything yet about John's possibly going into the Hall of Fame. John was eligible that year. Jack said, "Hold on. Wait a minute. . . . Yeah, he's going to be inducted."

It wasn't an hour later that I got a call at Liberty National Bank, where I had been hired to build their security program, and it was John. He said to me, "Coach, I want you to do me a favor. I want you to be my presenter when I go to the Hall of Fame in Canton, Ohio." There have been very few times in my life that I have been speechless, but that was one of them.

I didn't know about it at the time, but Sandy (Unitas, John's second wife) told me later, that there had been bets at the bars all over Baltimore as to who was going to be John's presenter. Typical John; he was unpredictable, just like he had been on the football field. I promise you nobody had their money on me. "Frank? Frank who? Who *is* that guy?"

I told John I would be more than happy to do it, but that I first wanted to go to Coach Camp and make sure he had no problem with it, that there wouldn't be any hard feelings. I got into my car and drove over to see Coach Camp, who by this time had had a heart attack and was now working as an assistant athletic director at Louisville. He was out at practice helping the quarterbacks.

So I went to the football field and got him aside and told him what was going on. He said, "Oh, Coach, that's great." I said, "Well, do you think I ought to do it?" he said, "Absolutely, go ahead and do it," and so I phoned John back and said, "Hell, yes, I'll do it."

GITSCHIER recalls the Hall of Fame induction ceremony in Canton, Ohio:

That was a great experience. We got there on Thursday, and there was a cocktail party that day. At one point, I saw some guy with gray hair and in a green coat go over and say something to John, and John pointed at me. The guy said just loud enough for a bunch of people to hear, "I'm the guy in charge of television and the presenters. We've had a lot of blowhards in here before who have talked for ten or fifteen minutes. Well, you've got five minutes to introduce John Unitas."

I looked right at John and said, "Fellow, you can put it in your book; I'll be done in five minutes."

My wife and three sons were there with me. There was a halo around Canton, and it was raining everywhere. Frank Jr. had his umbrella with him, and I told him to time me during my speech and at four minutes forty-five seconds into my speech to stick his umbrella up into the air. When the time came, he was just getting ready to put his umbrella up when I finished. Good timing. It came out perfect.

The next day they had a parade, and we were in open-air cars. People were lined up all along the route. At one point, the parade stopped, and this young couple came up to the car. They had a baby with them; it looked like it had just come out of the womb, it was still red. They came running out while the car was stopped to my side of the car with John seated next to me, and they yelled, "Just touch him, John, just touch him!" And John touched the baby.

After the parade was over, we went inside, and there were people everywhere wanting autographs. I go outside and run into a family. The wife looks at me and says, "Aren't you Mr. Gitschier?" I said, "Yes." She said, "Well, we'll from Sharpsville," which is right near Sharon, Pennsylvania, where I'm from, "and we tried to get Johnny's autograph, but we failed. We came all the way from Sharpsville. Mr. Gitschier, we know who you are and what you can do. Could you get us an autograph?"

I said, "Let me see what I can do." So I go back outside, and John's eating there with Sandy, John Jr., and Helen. I said, "John, I hate to ask you this, but there are some people here who really want to see you and get your autograph." John came outside and even had his picture taken with the father before he went back inside. Just think how many guys in Johnny's shoes wouldn't even have come outside in the first place. He did, and it was no problem with him at all,

and this was only about an hour before the ceremony
started.

<hr />

*Long after he had retired from the game, Unitas was
still fighting on behalf of hundreds of NFL retirees who
were getting little in the way of a pension and health
benefits.* **GITSCHIER:**

Another thing John was big on was retirement pay and
health benefits for retired NFL players. He led the charge. I
once had an aide to a senator call me and he had heard about
some of the things John was doing for these guys, some of
whom are in wheelchairs or otherwise disabled, and they
were getting only about two hundred dollars a month or
something. John has led that resurrection to try and help
them, and finally, this year, they increased the pension for
those guys.

<hr />

GITSCHIER *is doing his part as chairman of the Johnny
Unitas Golden Arm Educational Foundation:*

I met NFL commissioner Paul Tagliabue at John's funeral,
where I gave the eulogy. About a week and a half later, I
wrote a personal letter to Commissioner Tagliabue telling
him that our foundation had lost its breadwinner, and that
we were going to individuals, corporations, and foundations
to see if we can help generate some funds for these kids, to
give something back to the community in Louisville that
had accepted him here.

The letter arrived at the commissioner's office on the day
before they were having a meeting with the NFL charities.
Joe Browne runs the NFL charities, and I got a letter back

from him and they gave us twenty-five thousand dollars. That's the kind of thing keeping us going now.

Before, John would go to West Virginia and play in Sam Huff's golf tournament, and Huff would come here for John Unitas's dinner or whatever it would be. That's how we did it.

***

MICHAEL DELLIS, *a lifelong Baltimore-area resident and Colts fan, is the proprietor of Michael's Café, a popular restaurant in Timonium, Maryland, just north of Baltimore. Michael's was one of Unitas's favorite eating places, and he and Dellis became good friends over the years:*

What's ironic is that even with all the memorabilia I have lining the walls in here and all those times I have gotten John to sign things for other people, I never took the time to have him really sign anything for me, other than one helmet and a chronological poster I have hanging up on a wall behind the bar. We just never got around to doing anything else with him, and I guess I always figured there would be time for that.

***

DELLIS *gives his take on the Colts and what Unitas meant to sports fans throughout Baltimore and beyond:*

The Colts are still such a big part of this city's identity. They always will be. Even when you go to the Ravens game now, outside the stadium you see that big statue of John that was unveiled last year right after his death (in 2002). When you see John, you can't help but think *Colts*. I see people all the time who just walk over and touch the statue before they go in the game. They touch it again when they leave. And these

PHOTO COURTESY OF RICHARD SAMMIS

Johnny U, less than a year before his death, kicks back.

are young kids, too, so young that they were born years after John retired from football.

I have a nephew who has lived his entire life in Madison, Wisconsin, and he is a diehard John Unitas fan. I got him to meet Johnny when his family came down to visit one time, and he was thirteen or fourteen at the time. He could tell you *everything* in the world about John Unitas—stats, everything. He's a Green Bay Packers fan, sure, but he's even more a John Unitas fan. That's the kind of impact on people that John had over and over and over, even with people who have never lived near Baltimore nor got to see him play.

It seems like only yesterday that the Colts lived here. Now you hear talk about them possibly moving from Indianapolis to Saint Louis or Los Angeles. It's a shame that has to happen.

Rosemary Rausch *has worked at Michael's Café for seven years, most recently as a bartender, and recalls that Unitas would usually eat his lunch at the bar:*

One thing he would talk about a lot, because it was very important to him, was the old, old Colts, the ones who didn't have any, or very little, benefits from the NFL. They never got anything close to the big money these guys are getting today. John was always going around, looking to get help for these old guys—a better pension and more health benefits.

He would say, "There are a lot of guys out there who played the game when I did that are in a lot worse shape than I am." Some of those guys were in wheelchairs or otherwise somewhat debilitated and it looked like they had lived a hard life. Many of them didn't have any or enough money to help themselves out.

I would tell him, "I always feel so bad about your pain." He would say, "Ahhh, that's nothing. I have some buddies who are a lot worse off than I am." He felt that these were the guys who started the sport, who gave it a chance to be what it is now, and they should be duly compensated and taken care of. They are the ones who started the whole American love affair with pro football.

These guys loved playing football so much, they would take other jobs so that they could afford to keep playing.

Shirley Green, *on the loss of her brother:*

I was amazed when we went to his funeral. The people in Baltimore just loved him. The emotion that we saw on the drive to the church just touched me. He's an icon there. Seeing that made me so proud of the way that he lived.

ROSEMARY RAUSCH *is frequently reminded of John Unitas:*

John's son Chad comes in here a lot, and he's the spittin' image of his dad, right down to the crew cut. He looks soooo much like John, it's scary. He's even a little hunched over and saunters just like his dad did.

We were always encouraging Chad to do well in school, and he came back in after he had completed his degree at Towson State. He was really proud of that, and we reminded him that John was proud of him, too, that he was looking down smiling on him.

TOM MATTE *goes deeper with the Unitas legacy:*

The Baltimore Colts were the first "America's Team." John put the NFL back on the map with that performance in the 1958 NFL Championship Game. People could relate to a guy like John Unitas. He was everybody's dream of what he wanted to be when he grew up; he's the type of guy you would look at and think, *If he can do it, why can't I do it?*

John set such a cool example—he always kept his composure. He was also the master of the two-minute offense. People call the West Coast offense a new thing, but that's a bunch of bull, because we had that same offense back in 1957, which was our two-minute offense.

You can't put a price tag on the impact that John had on pro football, the state of Maryland, and the Baltimore community. He's probably one of the biggest assets this state ever had.

Baltimore is an old, old town; it's old-time, and John is in everybody's household here, the way he touched so many lives.

ERNIE ACCORSI, *on the essence of Johnny U:*

I had a quote I used when he died. Some people said they didn't understand it, and others said it was the greatest quote on leadership they had ever heard.

"The greatest definition of leadership that I have ever seen was John Unitas walking onto the team bus on the road."

What I meant by that is that when you're on the road, you're always a little more jittery. You're in hostile territory, and it's just different. And you're all together, when at home you're all arriving in separate cars or whatever. On the road, all of a sudden John Unitas gets onto the bus, and you know everything is going to be okay. "He's on our side."

Phil Rizzuto said a similar thing about Joe DiMaggio. He said, "In the most critical situations, I look over my shoulder and see DiMaggio in center field, and I know everything is going to turn out okay."

John just gave you that confidence. On top of everything, everyone knew what a great person he was.

5

UNITAS WE STAND

In 1979 John Unitas was inducted into the Pro Football Hall of Fame. During his eighteen-year career, seventeen of them with the Colts, Johnny U completed 2,830 passes for more than 40,000 yards, threw 290 touchdown passes, had three years of 3,000 or more passing yards, earned three each NFL Player of the Year and MVP Awards, was selected for ten Pro Bowls, was picked NFL Player of the Decade for the 1960s, and was named Greatest Player in the First Fifty Years of Pro Football. His record of forty-seven consecutive games with at least one touchdown pass is now more than forty years old and has never been seriously threatened. He also played on three Colts teams that won a league championship.

But those numbers, impressive as they are, don't come close to painting a complete portrait of Unitas. Leave that to the dozens of people who knew him best as they offer a scattershot look at a genuine American sports hero, stooped shoulders and all.

One of the things boys did growing up in the forties and fifties when they weren't playing ball was to put on the gloves for some friendly backyard sparring. **RON PETRELLI,** *who lived in John's neighborhood, remembers Unitas as a tough boxer:*

Kids back then always used to have a set of boxing gloves lying around. We'd put the gloves on once in a while and fool around in the backyard. I had three brothers, and we used to box all the time. They would punch me around pretty good.

I liked boxing and was even thinking about getting into the Golden Gloves. But my brother knew a local pro and got him to spar with me, and this guy banged me around pretty good. That's when I decided that maybe this isn't really what I wanted to do.

I think John could have been a decent boxer, but I don't think he could have been a pro.

CLARK WOOD, *the former Louisville coach, recalls how regretful the Steelers later were for having cut Unitas in 1955:*

When the Pittsburgh people looked at John, they sent a young scout to look at him, and he went back to them, really recommending John to them. After they drafted John, he went up there. I'm not really sure what happened, except that they released him. I saw him soon after that and asked him what had happened, if he had looked bad in a scrimmage or something. He said, "No, I thought I did a helluva job. In fact on the day they released me, I had had one of the greatest days throwing the ball that I had ever had."

After John had gone on to the Colts and started playing well there, that same scout from Pittsburgh came by one time. As he walked into our office, he took his hat off and just threw it in the door, onto the floor. I asked him why he did that, and he said, "Well, I had always heard that when you go somewhere, you should first throw your hat in the door, and if they don't want you there, they'll throw it back out. But when you didn't do it, I came on in."

He went in and talked to Coach (Frank) Camp, and told Coach, "I'm going to do something for you because of the way Pittsburgh treated John." This guy had been a high school coach in Pittsburgh. "When I left there, there was this kid coming along, a freshman fullback, and he turned out to be a heckuva football player. I'm going to recruit that guy and bring him down here, and you don't have to do a darn thing." That running back turned out to be Ken Porco, who would become the fullback on our team that won the 1958 Sun Bowl. It was a form of payback.

FRANK GITSCHIER:

One of my favorite John Unitas trivia questions is to ask what uniform number he wore in high school, at Louisville, with the Bloomfield Rams, with the Pittsburgh Steelers, with the Colts, and then with the San Diego Chargers. The one that stumps everybody is the Bloomfield Rams' number. Nobody's gotten that yet.

At Saint Justin's, he wore eighteen; at Louisville, sixteen; with the Steelers, fourteen; nineteen with both the Colts and the Chargers; and forty-five with the Bloomfield Rams.

ALEX HAWKINS *takes a stab at explaining why he and Unitas got along so well, even though they didn't appear to have much in common:*

I got along with him wonderfully well, which proves that in some cases opposites do attract. John and I were best of friends. I think I represented something that he would have liked to have had in him, but he was just too responsible and it wasn't his nature. He got a kick out of some of the goofy things I did.

I never saw John have a drink of whiskey in his life. He would sometimes run from one bar to another with me, but he would be there and do it just to appease me. He'd drink a beer every now and then, but never any of the hard stuff.

ROSEMARY RAUSCH, *the bartender at Michael's Café, knew when Unitas was coming for lunch even before walked through the front door:*

You knew when he was coming even before he got inside because you could hear him whistling on his way in, and he'd be whistling on his way out. He was a beautiful whistler. No particular song. He called me Rosebud because he had heard that my dad called me that.

John would have lunch here three or four days a week. He was still traveling a lot, right up to the time he passed away. He was going all over the country making appearances for this and that, such as charity golf tournaments. He would sit at the bar and people would come up to him a lot, wanting an autograph, and he was so gracious.

It never bothered him. He would put his sandwich down, and his soup might get cold, but he would sit patiently and listen to them say what they had to say and

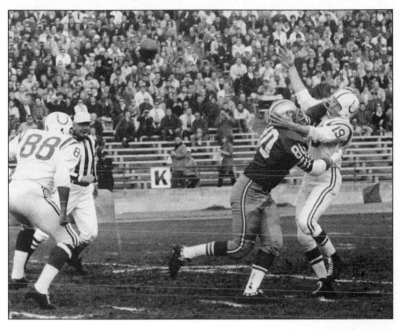

Getting rid of the ball right before getting clobbered was a Unitas trademark. Here he throws downfield just as Stan Hindman of the San Francisco Forty-niners makes contact in a 1966 game at Kezar Stadium.

then he would sign anything they put in front of him. He must have signed at least a hundred footballs for me, because people were always asking me to do that for them.

John knew the names of all the regulars here, and he would know when somebody had left or when somebody new had just come in for the first time. He would meet someone for the first time and ask them things to find out a little bit about them, and then he would remember everything the next time you came in. "How's your mom doing?" Stuff like that. Very personable.

LoANN DELLIS, *wife of Michael's Café owner Michael Dellis:*

We would see him three or four times a week, and you took for granted that he's always going to be coming around. You get to thinking that he's going to be around here forever.

He would come and eat lunch, and he wouldn't stay long, maybe forty-five minutes. He wasn't one to linger. He would just sit there, drink his milk, and eat his meal, and sign autographs if anyone asked. We would talk with him, and often it was about something other than football. And he had a wonderful sense of humor, very even keel.

Lots of times he would come to lunch with his son Chad. Chad still comes in occasionally, although not as frequently as he used to. Chad always resembled his dad, but when he got a crew cut, the resemblance was incredible.

RICHARD SAMMIS *recalls how John and the San Diego Chargers, or at least San Diego, were not a good fit:*

John hated it in San Diego. He didn't like the lifestyle—he's a more conservative-type person. San Diego was flashy, rich, and overflowing. That's not his deal.

Considering the career he'd had in Baltimore, he never got his deal here, the one where he gets to say goodbye to the fans.

LENNY MOORE *and Unitas were teammates for more than a decade, although that didn't make them bosom buddies. Moore elaborates:*

I could tell you nothing about the personal side of John because we only knew each other on the football field and in the locker room. We never socialized together, not with the black-and-white atmosphere at that time.

Blacks couldn't go here, blacks couldn't go there, they couldn't go to the movies. There were a lot of restaurants we couldn't go to and a lot of hotels we couldn't stay in. That just cut us blacks off from the rest of the team. We were restricted to the black section of town. At training camp, blacks were pretty much confined to the dormitories because there were so few places for us to go to. Couldn't do anything.

I had a little area that I would go to just across the highway from training camp. There was a duck pond that I would go to all by myself. It was my quiet place where I would work myself through all of that. I might break some bread and throw some pieces to the ducks or just sit there and think about things. I don't know if I can just describe how I felt as anger—I wish I had the verbiage to describe how one feels, the pain that you never lose from being disengaged, or disarmed, so to speak. Ostracized. Even when you want to socialize, you can't socialize. We had no outlet for us to get to know one another.

Even when you were with the other guys, you knew you could only take conversation to a certain limit. In listening to the white guys talk, you could feel the conversation getting to the point where someone would make a snide remark or a little putdown, even if it wasn't thought out. It would happen because of the way people talk. That's why I was never hanging around with white players when they were drinking. They might say something like, "Hey, you're just as good as we are," which to them might sound like praise, but which to blacks come across as a putdown.

One of the few areas we could go to where we could freely mix was Minnesota, when we went up there to play the Vikings. That was for the few hours we had before bed

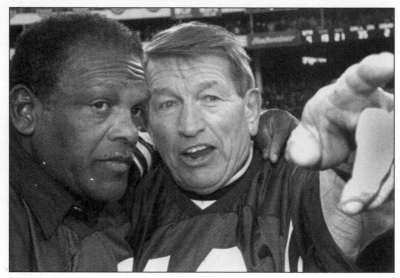

*A couple of Hall of Fame vets and former Colts teammates, Lenny Moore and
Unitas, reunite during a Baltimore Ravens game in December 1997.*

check on the night before the game. You still had to perform
at 100 percent on the field, although there might be
moments where your mind would drift, and you had to pull
yourself back to the matter at hand. It's no wonder Jackie
Robinson died in his early fifties.

*Old societal ways were slow to change, as **MOORE**
found out in 1981 when he and another former Colts
player, Milt Davis, also an African American, attended
a get-together of his old Colts teammates:*

Milt Davis came to town and asked me if I had bumped into
any of the players or knew what they were up to, and I asked
him if he wanted to go to this alumni thing. He said yeah.

Very seldom did I go to any of these alumni things for said reasons. Going to those things was a question of "When is it coming?" Anyway, Milt and I went.

Unitas was there. Donovan. (Dick) Szymanski—all the guys. We were milling around, talking and chatting, asking about each other's family, keeping things on that level. We had a little bite to eat. After about an hour and a half of this, I said to Milt, "Well, Pop, you about ready to go?" He said, "Yeah," and at that point someone got up and said, "Okay, before anybody goes, you've got to say something, whatever you want to say."

A couple of other guys had already left. Milt said something brief about his now living in California and not getting much of an opportunity to keep up with the guys, and how much he appreciated getting together with everyone. Milt kept it in that vein.

I got up and said, "You know what, men? We keep B.S.-ing each other. All these years that we've been together, I've never been to your house and you've never invited me to your house," pointing to different guys, "but I've invited some of you to my house. But we've never done anything socially together. That's a damn shame. I wish I would have gotten to know you guys, but I don't know you. Not really. Oh, yeah, I know you as a football player, but that's not what I'm talking about. I don't know you and you don't know me. That's a sad commentary, fellows, after all these years, yet we B.S. each other as if we do."

I looked over and saw Weeb and Unitas sitting next to each other. I wanted to make eye contact with them, but they were looking down. You could hear a pin drop. But I do care about these guys.

---

*Longtime NFL official **Norm Schachter** worked Super Bowl V between the Cowboys and Colts. He* *remembers a controversial play in the game in which a Unitas pass bounced off the hands of receiver Ed Hinton downfield into the hands of John Mackey for a seventy-five-yard touchdown play. The question was whether the ball had touched Dallas defensive back Mel Renfro's hands in going from Hinton to Mackey. After conferring with his back judge, Schachter ruled that the ball had indeed grazed Renfro's hands and, therefore, the play stood as a touchdown. Two years later, Schachter was reminded of that play during a chance encounter that included Unitas. Schachter:*

I was in San Diego to give the Chargers a rule talk before the season opened. Johnny Unitas, who had been the quarterback for the Colts in that game, and Pettis Norman, a receiver from Dallas in Super Bowl V, were now teammates on the San Diego team. They were sitting next to each other when I got up to give the rules talk.

Before I could start, Pettis Norman piped up: "Norm, you still owe me seven thousand five hundred dollars. Renfro never touched that ball."

Winners of the Super Bowl received $15,000. Losers got $7,500. Pettis Norman wanted that $7,500 difference. I looked at him, then looked at Unitas, who was on his left. "I don't owe it to you. I didn't get the money. I get the same fee no matter who wins. Unitas got a winning share. He's right next to you. Why doesn't he give it to you?"

Unitas put his hand in his pocket, took out his money clip, and turned toward Pettis Norman. "Pettis, how much did you say it was?" [1]

SCHACHTER *estimates he worked more than twenty games involving rivals Green Bay and Baltimore. He*

*recalls one particular moment in one of those classic
contests that revolved around Unitas and a question-
able fumble call:*

John Unitas . . . was the best. That's what I think. And
I've worked them all for twenty-two years. A smart quarterback is always thinking. That's what I liked about
John Unitas. He was thinking all the time. He was a
gentleman, but that didn't stop him from trying to out-
smart the referee.

Unitas was hit from the blind side as he was setting up
to throw a pass. If his hand was coming down and the ball
dropped out of his hand, then it was an incomplete pass.
If the ball was knocked out of his hand before his hand
was coming down, then it was a fumble. I had to give it a
good look and to be in position. I did, and I was. Just as
Unitas was hit from the side, the ball dropped out of his
hand. Just as soon as the ball dropped from his hand,
Unitas brought his right hand forward. It was a bang-bang
play.

I ruled it a fumble and let the play develop. The Packers
recovered. Unitas rushed me and said, "My hand was coming down. It was an incomplete pass. No way a fumble if my
hand was coming down."

I agreed with Unitas. "That's right, John, your hand was
coming down. But the ball has to be in it."

Unitas smiled and walked away. He was thinking all the
time. The (Baltimore) fans let me have it. They didn't see
Unitas smile. And they weren't thinking.[2]

*Longtime Unitas friend **RICHARD SAMMIS** remembers
how Johnny U's right hand had become pretty much
useless in his later years:*

Super Bowl V against the Dallas Cowboys in January 1971 had its rough moments for Unitas, but the Colts prevailed anyway, 16-13.

His hand wasn't as much arthritic but damaged from hitting it against helmets so many times. The nerves inside were just shattered. He couldn't pick this little cell phone up. He had no squeezing power. He went to the hospital to get treatments to help strengthen it. But the first treatment gave him a ministroke.

He would never complain. He figured out how to write with that hand, and his signature was perfect. When we played golf, he put the club in his hand and wrapped the Velcro from his golf glove around his hand and the club because he couldn't grip it. He always found a way.[3]

In the last years of his life, Unitas's right hand was so wracked by osteoarthritis, that he needed someone to cut his meat for him. **GENE UPSHAW,** *executive director of the NFL Players Association, credits Unitas with helping the NFLPA improve pension benefits for older players. Upshaw:*

He could have been out playing golf, but he stayed involved with us. I'm going to miss his friendship. He understood what the fight was all about. When we got this last extension this past year, it was like a 50 percent improvement. That's when we made two hundred dollars a month in benefits for an accredited season. We spent $110 million this past year on these retired guys. John was getting $85,000, $86,000 in pension this past year.[4]

RICHARD SAMMIS *recalls how inventive Unitas could be when it came to playing quality golf despite the condition of his right hand:*

When John first went back to playing golf after his hand had gotten to be real bad, the first thing he did was get thicker grips for his clubs so he wouldn't have to squeeze so hard. His right hand, though, he couldn't squeeze at all. He couldn't pick a pen up with his right hand. No way.

One day we were playing golf at Chestnut Ridge, and we started talking about getting something to hold his hands together on the club. I live on the eighteenth hole at Chestnut Ridge and I said, "John, I have an idea. Stay right here. I'm going home." I drove home and brought from home one of those elastic knee braces. We cut this thing and cut it some more to fashion something we could wrap around his hand.

We got to doing this, trying to get what was left of this brace somehow wrapped, and we started laughing so hard out on the golf course that John had to sit back down in the cart. Tears were coming down his face. We called it "the Unitas Girdle." It didn't work. But what it did do was give him an idea.

He got another golf club and had Velcro sewn into the grip, and then had a long Velcro strap made for his hand, so that when he put the club in his hand, he could wrap the long Velcro strap around his hand and the club, and he could make it as tight or as loose as he wanted. That held his hand on the club, and to the day that he passed away, that's how he played golf. John had it down to where he could do this in a matter of seconds.

When he putted, he just took it off because he didn't need it. He would just unwrap the Velcro strap and he would be putting, with this big strip of Velcro just hanging down. It looked funny, but it didn't matter to John because it worked.

His golf game had gone from where he could shoot in the low eighties to where, with his bad hand, he would be shooting about 110 or 115. When he learned how to properly wrap his hand to the club, John was back to scoring in the low eighties again, and that was phenomenal. He taught himself how to do that. I got him on the right track, and he figured out how to make it better and how to make it work.

John never complained, although he hated playing in the rain. The wind didn't bother him as much. When the rain came down, he was looking for the clubhouse.

Although Unitas hated playing golf in the rain, there were times when he did so for a good cause. **SAMMIS:**

I had a daughter, Diane, who died at age twenty-seven of leukemia. I started a golf tournament in her honor—that was ten years ago—and John never missed it. We started the tournament to raise money to give to the research doctors to come up with a cure for leukemia.

One time it was raining cats and dogs for the tournament. John was on the eighth hole when I caught up to him, and he looked at me and said, "Richard, it's a good thing that you have good friends." We canceled it at the end of nine holes because it was raining so hard.

John was the kind of guy who, if something else came up on the same day of the tournament that would pay him fifteen thousand dollars, he would not do it. John was committed to the golf tournament. That's the way he is.

In the eight years of the tournament, we have raised over a half million dollars, and it all goes to the Johns Hopkins Research Center.

ERNIE ACCORSI, *the former Colts P.R. director, never ceased being amazed by Unitas's humility:*

I can remember his being startled at some of the things I would ask him to do. Like at the 1971 Super Bowl, I told him, "We need to have special press conferences for you." Usually, they had those only for the head coaches. He looked at me like I was from another planet. I said to him, "Do you have a clue how big you are." He just looked at me bewildered.

I don't think until near the end, when they unveiled the statue at Louisville, and he knew he had another one coming in Baltimore, that he realized how big he was or what he meant, not only to Baltimore and Maryland but to the entire country.

JOE HORRIGAN, *vice president of the Pro Football Hall of Fame:*

Some celebrities, if you had a line drawing of eyeglasses, fuzzy eyebrows, and a cigar, you'd know it was Groucho Marx. In football, if you had a drawing of a pair of hightops and a crew cut, it would be only one person: Johnny Unitas. He was a caricature of football in the fifties. [5]

REGGIE BETHEA, *a teammate of Unitas at Louisville, recalls how Unitas had no trouble just being one of the guys:*

Harold (Bethea, his brother) and I were roommates. Every so often, maybe it was once every two or three months, Johnny would come and knock on our door, where Harold and I might have been studying instead of being somewhere else drinking or something like most everyone else did.

After he knocked, Johnny would come walking in, sit down on the edge of one of the beds, and ask us, "How are you guys doing?" We'd chew the fat for a while, and then Johnny might suggest that we go get a cup of coffee. There was a little place nearby called Cardinal Inn where we would go have a cup of coffee and sit there looking at one another, not saying a whole lot. We thought he would do this kind of thing only with us, but we found out in time that he did this with a lot of the guys. He would contact even the lowest player like this.

I would send Johnny a Christmas card every year, and every now and then he would poke his head out into the world and maybe give me a call to see how things were. Several years before he died, after my wife Barbara and I had moved to Arizona, we got a phone call early one morning with Barbara still in bed. She answered the phone, and this guy on the other end said, "Hello. Barbara?" Well, she didn't know who it was because she was sleepy.

He said, "What are you doing?" She said, "I'm just lying here in bed." And Johnny goes, "Well, where's Reggie?" She said, "I don't know where he's at." And he said, "Now, Barbara, you're not supposed to be lying in bed at this time of morning without Reggie there with you. I think I'm going to need to talk to Reggie about this."

Then I got on the phone with him, and we talked just as if he had walked into the room, like longtime friends really comfortable with one another, just as if we were back in school. He would call like this every two or three years, even as busy as he was. He called us not because we were best friends, but simply because he remembered us. He just wanted to touch base. That's the kind of guy he was—he never forgot a friend.

REGGIE BETHEA *remembers one particular scenario at Louisville in which Unitas went above and beyond the call of duty to help out a teammate:*

I remember one time when there was a prom, and Johnny and I were both hurt, so we were just staying up in our respective rooms taking it easy. Besides, Johnny, I think, was engaged at the time and I was going steady with the young woman, Barbara, that I would end up marrying. John's arm was hurting, and I was propped up in bed with an injured knee.

Johnny came down to see me and to talk with me, and sometime that night we got a call to the dorm telling us that the mother of one of the other guys had just passed away. Johnny turned to me and said, "Hey, Reggie, let's go get him"—this other guy was at the prom—"and let's be the ones to tell him what happened."

As I recall, Johnny had the keys to some car; it might even have been his, I don't remember. We drove down into

Louisville to where the prom was going on. We went in and Johnny went up to the guy, and it was really neat how Johnny handled things from there. I don't remember who the player was, only that Johnny gently pulled him away from the dance and told him what had happened. The guy was obviously stricken by the sad news, so Johnny took him into a room off to the side and talked to the guy for a while, consoling him. We took the guy back to the dorm, then Johnny made arrangements for him to get home on an airplane so he could go home and be with his family.

Johnny did most of the handling through all this—I was just there helping out as best I could. To see Johnny in action, with such compassion for a guy he really didn't know all that well, was really something. He was a special person. Because of his talent, Johnny was recognized, but because of how he treated people, he was respected. My own mom died before I got out of college, and Johnny helped me out both monetarily and spiritually.

This guy had a feel for people, and he never forgot a friend. Some time after graduation, after I had moved back home to Birmingham, Alabama, Johnny was on his way to New Orleans to meet with the Los Angeles Rams coach. Johnny was going to go talk to him about playing football, and this was before Johnny ended up with the Colts.

On his way down, Johnny stopped by our house to talk with me. That meant a lot to me, that a guy would take time out from such an important trip related to his career to come see me, someone who wasn't what you would call one of Johnny's best friends.

ALEX HAWKINS, *on going out to eat with an unassuming Unitas one time after a game in Los Angeles:*

John and I were sitting in a restaurant having dinner with Max Baer Jr. and Robert Mitchum's son, Jim, when Hollywood columnist Louella Parsons approached our table. I had no idea how important Louella was, and Unitas was without interest in such matters. He did not like pretense of any kind. John loved children and would stand in the rain, sign autographs, and pose for pictures for as long as they wanted, but he would not have driven fifty miles to meet the president of the United States.

When Louella approached our table, Mitchum and Baer almost turned the table over to greet her. Louella Parsons addressed John from the rear. "Mr. Unitas, I have always been a big fan of yours," she gushed, "and I would like to take this opportunity to meet you."

Looking straight up and over his head, he replied, "Sure, Louella, sit your ass down and have a beer." Louella dropped her cane and did a 9.5 sprint out of the restaurant. John's response might appear to have been rude, but he was so untouched by success and so unimpressed with stardom for himself or anyone else, that it was just a natural thing for him to say. [6]

LENNY LYLES:

I remember one time when Tom Matte was playing quarterback because of an injury to John. A bunch of us out on the field were giving suggestions to Tom about what he should do next, what play to call, and finally this one official standing by told us to shut up and to let Tom call the play. This ref wasn't pulling for us, but it was obvious he just couldn't stand hearing any more of all our jabbering. I think the deal for us was that because John was hurt, the rest of us needed to step up and help Tom out, when in fact he was fine on his own.

RAYMOND BERRY *recalls one of the last times he saw his former quarterback before Unitas passed away, and he still had some questions that needed answering:*

We stayed in touch over the years and got together every now and then. In the year before he died, I had probably the two best visits with him that I had had in the whole thirty years before that.

He and Sandy came out here to Colorado to attend a graduation ceremony at one of the universities around here and then they spent a couple days with me and Sally. We live in the mountains just west of Denver. It's a beautiful area.

John and I had a great time just hashing over old things. In fact, Sally saw all of this and said, "You guys ought to write a book together and call it *Unitas and Berry*."

Then I saw him when we did a promotion together for Wal-Mart down in Arkansas. We were there for a couple days together and had a real good time.

Before we got together during their trip to Colorado, I had put together a list of things I was going to ask John about, things I've been curious about over the years. One of them had to do with the two-minute drive against the Giants. All my years of coaching had given me a new appreciation for that two-minute drive. One of the things I was curious about was why John did what he did during that two-minute drive, when we had so far to go with just one timeout left.

On a third-and-ten, John hit Lenny Moore for an eleven-yard gain, and I'm pretty sure that's when John used the last timeout. That's when he came to me three times in a row on those inside pass plays. So when we got together years later, I asked him, "Why did you come to me three times in a row?" And he said, "I figured you would catch them."

*Although **BERRY** would go on to become a coach after his playing days, it was a creer move that Unitas never made:*

I don't know if John was cut out to be a coach. The tolerance it takes to be a coach can be really high. I doubt if he would have been able to enjoy coaching very much.

Philadelphia Daily News *sportswriter Dick Jerardi was a teenager in junior high in Baltimore when he first met Unitas—while hitchhiking home on city streets:*

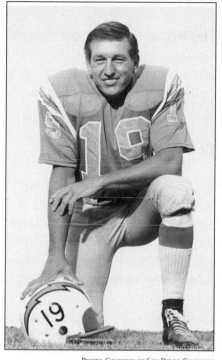

PHOTO COURTESY OF SAN DIEGO CHARGERS

Unitas ended his football career with the San Diego Chargers.

In my memory, a blue Lincoln pulled over. Everything's bigger when you're a kid, but it definitely was not a compact. The driver motioned me into the car, and I looked in and said to myself, "That's Johnny Unitas." He gave me a pleasant smile, and I was too stunned to speak. He knew that I knew who he was, and he knew I was petrified. He humored me for a few miles, until I had the presence of mind to ask him to let me off near my neighborhood. I ran home and told my brothers about it, but I'm not sure any of them believed me. [7]

UNITAS, *on sportswriters in general:*

Sportswriters always seemed to make some things more important than they should be. [8]

ALEX HAWKINS:

I still get asked about John all the time. John wasn't a deep person—to him, life was black and white; things were very simple. He didn't out-think himself.

Adds **RICHARD SAMMIS:**

One of John's favorite statements was "No big deal." No matter what, even if it was bigger than a big deal to me or someone else. Then again, if Johnny Unitas wasn't worried about it, why should I be?

If Unitas had emotional highs and lows, he rarely showed them. **ERNIE ACCORSI:**

John once said, "I only get emotional over kids and animals. I don't get emotional over football games."

John Unitas as baby-sitter? You bet. **CLAUDIA GRIMM,** *who came to know the younger Unitas family while sitting around the baby pool at Hillendale Country Club, watching their kids, asked John and Sandy to be the godparents of her daughter Molly when she was three*

weeks old. One time, Sandy offered to baby-sit so
Claudia could go do some things. Claudia Grimm:

I was gone for five hours, and when I returned home, John was
sitting in the den, with Molly in his arms. I asked about Sandy,
and he said something had come up. I must have had a look on
my face, because he said, "You think I can't handle a baby?" He
had given her a bottle, changed her diaper, played with her.
Yes, John was a man's man, but there was a softer side to him.
There was never a time when he didn't have time for children.[9]

SHIRLEY GREEN, *John's younger sister:*

When we got together with John, he would take off his
shoes, and kick back and relax with us, talking about family
and rarely about football.

Unitas also pulled baby-sitting duty for the Frank
Gitschier family while he was at Louisville. **GITSCHIER:**

John would baby-sit for Mary and me sometimes. You couldn't
do that today, it would be against NCAA rules, but I paid him
out of our own money. Mary and I might go out to eat and then
downtown to the Armory to see a hockey game, or something
like that, and John would sit with our kids. He was terrific.

Former Louisville coach **CLARK WOOD:**

John was real loyal. I remember going to a Colts game one
time in the sixties, and after the game going down to an
area outside the locker room to see if I could see either

John or Lenny Lyles. I got down to the gate, but was told by a guard there that there was no chance I could see either one of them.

A little later someone opened the locker room door and I looked in and saw John standing there, surrounded by six to eight reporters. I'll be darned if John didn't happen to look out and see me standing out there. He told the reporters to give him a second, and he came out and talked to my wife, Polly, and me for about five minutes. That's the kind of person he was. He certainly wasn't one of those guys struttin' around and braggin'. If you didn't recognize him, you wouldn't have known that he was John Unitas.

TOM MATTE:

I never saw John not sign an autograph. A couple of years ago we were down in Birmingham, Alabama, playing in a corporate golf tournament. Others there included Kenny Stabler, Billy Kilmer, Roman Gabriel, and Unitas. When John came walking down the hall, word would just sort of spread. "That's John Unitas!" It was amazing how people revered him, and he deserved it. He was a special guy.

John always loved to play golf, and we had some great matches. He was always asking, "How many strokes are you going to give me?" I'd say, "Two," and he would go, "No, I want five a side." That's when I was playing pretty good, to about a six or seven handicap , and he would play to about fifteen to seventeen. We had a great time. Lots of laughs.

In his later years, we would get together for lunch sometimes over here (in the Timonium-Towson area, just north of Baltimore). He was always concerned for his children, from both families. He was a great father. He had a good life and was so down to earth as a person.

*MATTE recalls one very strange day on which both he
and Unitas ended up in the hospital:*

John and I were working out one time at a YMCA, I think it
was in 1970. We wanted to play racquetball but couldn't find
a court that was available. At one, there were a couple of
women playing and we knew who they and their husbands
were, so we asked them if we could join them for doubles.

At one point, John fell down at the front of the court. He
said, "Matte, you tripped me, you SOB!" I said, "How could I
trip you? I'm all the way back here." What had happened is
that he had torn his Achilles' tendon. You could see the
thing roll up just like a rubber band.

I helped him off the court and dropped him off at the
hospital. I have a restaurant that I then drove to. That afternoon, I got real sick and ended up at the doctor's office. I
was doubled up on the floor with cramps, and I was cough-
ing up some blood. They Demeroled me up and took me
down to the same hospital where John was. I was under
observation all night long.

It turned out that I had acute appendicitis. It was all twisted
around back in my pelvic area. So the two of us were in the hospital together, right across from each other. We drove the hospital crazy because we had everybody coming by to visit us,
bringing beer up to our rooms. It was like a bus station, even
fans and sportswriters, continual, for about twenty-four hours.
We were having a good time. Back then, the doctors didn't care
about our drinking beers, and you've got to remember, we
owned this town. We were both there about three or four days.

*MATTE also remembers how Unitas helped organize
"team meetings," over beers, of course:*

Judy and I had just gotten married. Every Friday we had a weigh-in, and after the weigh-in we would have a practice. After practice we always went to this little bar called Andy's.

It was around Christmastime, and my wife knew I would always come home a little late at night, and she didn't exactly know why. She wanted me to come home and do some Christmas shopping, and I told her I would get out early.

So this one night, I make the announcement to the other guys at the bar that I need to get going. Unitas and Gino Marchetti looked at me and asked where I was going. I said, "I gotta go home, to do some shopping with my wife." John said, "Call her up and tell her it's a team meeting." I called her and said, "Jude, I can't get home right now. We're having a team meeting." And she goes, "Oh, okay."

This went on for about ten years, and we'd go home half in the bag. You've got to remember, we really had to crash to make weight, and we figured we needed to drink beer afterward to replenish all those lost fluids. We would get twenty-five to thirty guys together for this, and that's how close we all were. We had the greatest time.

The most fun we had was when we went to training camp. We got away from all the responsibilities of home, and we were at boys' camp.

In his post-football career as a businessman, Unitas had his ups and downs, including a few failed businesses that he had a stake in. FRANK GITSCHIER says that whatever problems Unitas had, they were often rooted in his trustworthiness—even when it came to memorabilia. Gitschier:

We had had problems with Johnny signing things for guys who turned out to be professional memorabilia dealers. John

Jr. and I would both tell John to be careful about not doing too much of that. We realized that he was being taken. These guys have to be careful. I know when Bart Starr gives an autograph, he will personalize it—he won't give it to you with just his name. We didn't get John to do that until his later years—he would sign anything for anybody.

When John went to a restaurant with his family, the one thing he didn't like was seeing some guy with his family all looking at him. He'd say to me, "Coach, I know what they're wanting to do; they want an autograph. You know what they do? They wait until the food shows up, and then they come over." That bugged him, and that's about as bad a thing as I can say about John.

John was so trustworthy, to a point that it could be ridiculous. He had business partners who took advantage of him, including one guy he was sending money to for a business venture, only to find out after a while that something was wrong when someone from a produce or meat company supplying one of the restaurants he had bought into was calling him telling him they hadn't gotten paid in over a month.

John jumped on a plane to go down there and found out that his buddy had been at the racetrack, spending all of the money there. John had just turned the business over to a close personal friend of his and told him to "just send me the checks." John trusted people, and a lot of people took advantage of him.

RICHARD SAMMIS:

John had his name involved in a lot of businesses. The Golden Arm Restaurant. Then he and Bobby Boyd expanded into the Baby Doe's Mining Company, which was another restaurant in Towson. Then John got involved in some bowling alleys, a freight company, an electronics company. None of them really panned out. For example, something went wrong with the Golden Arm, where someone had misappropriated funds or something like that.

John was a very trusting guy. He would listen to you and help you, and then he got hurt in some of these ventures. He took some hits, but through some marketing of himself at card shows and things like that, he got back on his feet again. The day that he passed away was the day on which he and his family were closing on selling their big house with nineteen acres. That was really tough on Sandy, but she has done a marvelous job. She has picked up the pieces.

Tom Matte:

I think John covered himself pretty well with the bankruptcies that he had. I almost went into business with him at one time, and we even ended up competitors in the printed-circuit-board business. I'm pretty sure he ended up okay financially. He was a pretty smart guy, but he got screwed a couple of times.

One way to get John Unitas's goat was to tamper with his beloved Colts, and that's what owner Robert Irsay did, in the minds of Unitas and hordes of Colts fans, when he moved the franchise to Indianapolis in 1984.

Frank Gitschier:

John wasn't happy about that at all. In fact, John said, "They have no right to put the Colts' records in their book." That was his big thing. "We played in Baltimore, and that's where those records should stay." The Baltimore Colts played in Baltimore, and this is not the same team—these are the

Indianapolis Colts, so our records belong with the Ravens even though we didn't play with the Ravens.

RICHARD SAMMIS *saw Unitas as a guy without pretension:*

John was the kind of guy who would treat the man cleaning the floors of the hundred-story building the same way that he would treat the man who owned it. It was never too much to say hello to anyone. It was never too much to sign an autograph or speak nicely to whomever it was that came up to him.

John treated me as good as anyone could treat me, and he would have treated you the same way if he had met you. John was not the guy who would beep the horn at you if you didn't take off within three seconds after the light turned green.

SAMMIS *continues:*

I'm also good friends with Jim Palmer, but I hate baseball. It's too slow for me. I am really a football person, and remain involved with the Ravens today.

I have a TV commercial that we cut back in the mid-seventies that featured Palmer, John, and Bert Jones all together. We were selling Jeeps. Palmer had a line on introducing the Jeep, John had some lines about technical things, and then here comes Bert Jones down the middle with a big cowboy hat on. It was crazy and fun. You couldn't get three guys like that together in a commercial like that today. No way. They wouldn't do it.

John would learn his words, and he was never nervous. Bert's in there, the rookie so to speak, all full of vim and vigor, and then you've got the analyst in Jim Palmer. Jim's

AP/WIDE WORLD PHOTOS-CITIZENS VOICE, WARREN RUDA

Unitas at a July 2001 press conference in which he was announced as a part-owner of the Wilkes-Barre, Pennsylvania, team in the Arena Football League 2.

lips would be moving while John was speaking and it was the same deal when Bert spoke—Palmer had memorized all the lines, and it was so much fun.

SAMMIS remembers one time when he tried to engage Unitas in a discussion about football strategy:

One night, I don't remember what year it was, but it was after the Monday night radio show we had at the Golden Arm. It must have been almost two o'clock in the morning, and he and I had both been doing real good on the drinking side that night.

We were arguing over football. He was trying to draw a play on a wet napkin with a fine-point pen. You can just

imagine; the napkin was falling all apart. I'm arguing with
him, as he's drawing this play, as to who's going to cover who
and all that stuff. Finally, the paper is disintegrating, and he
looks up at me and says, "Why am I doing this for you?
You're the car man, I'm the football guy!" And that ended
the conversation.

*After the Colts were taken from Baltimore, it would be
some fifteen years before Unitas would again stand on
the sidelines of an NFL game in Baltimore. It took some
coaxing, but* **RICHARD SAMMIS** *finally was able to get
Unitas to go to a Ravens game, circa 1999. Sammis:*

It took me four years of trying, but I finally got John to get
out and go to some of the Ravens games. Eventually, John
would be on the sidelines for the games.

Ravens Coach Brian Billick had called me one time and
asked me to set up a lunch with John. So I did, and they had
a very good relationship develop out of that. Billick told me
once, with John right there, that, "When things get going
rough out here and you're still there on the sideline, I feel
like I have a chance. But if things are going rough and I look
over and you are gone, I know I'm done."

SAM HUFF:

I got to really know John when we went to Vietnam for
twelve days in 1966. The commissioner asked myself, Frank
Gifford, Willie Davis, and John to go. We got shot at, and
John never flinched. John was class. Nobody ever hit John
Unitas dirty. You respect the general. John was that.[10]

ALEX HAWKINS, with a touch of sarcasm, pays
homage to Unitas's good-role-model image:

A man cannot play the game of football without a clearly
defined philosophy to fall back on. Although John Unitas was
my hero, and I would gladly have killed for him, he would not
do as a role model. He was a moderate beer drinker and a
good husband and father. He would stop off and have a couple
of beers with us after practice, but afterwards he always went
home for dinner. I was looking for someone a little more
swashbuckling, someone that I could pattern myself after and
use to develop a philosophy about this game I was playing.[11]

RALPH GREEN, Unitas's brother-in-law, would take in
a Colts game whenever it was practical:

I remember one time going to one of John's Colts games, late
in his career, in which they played the Steelers, and
Pittsburgh won. After the game we were outside the dressing
room waiting for John to come out. There was this big ramp
beside us, and here comes big Bubba Smith, who had been
traded from the Colts to the Steelers, walking down the
ramp. Helen (John's mother) confronted him and said, "Now,
you knocked my boy down too many times." There she is,
looking up at Bubba towering over her, a bowler hat on her
head. And he looks down at her and says, "But ya know, Mrs.
Unitas, every time I knocks him down, I picks him up."

Offensive lineman **DAN SULLIVAN** played eleven
seasons with the Colts and recalls some cunning play-
calling by Unitas in a game against the Dallas Cowboys:

John would ask if anyone needed any help. My nemesis was Jethro Pugh, who was tall, rangy, and gave me all sorts of problems. In one of our games, I came out aggressive and was doing real well against him. (Left guard) Glenn Ressler was matched up against Bob Lilly, and you need help against him any day, which we tried to give. Two series later, Pugh got by me and leveled John a couple of times. (John) said, "Can't you block this guy?" He called a sucker play, what you would call a counter today. I pulled left, Jethro followed me, and Glenn came over and cleaned his clock. When you least expected a play, John would call it. [12]

ROSEMARY RAUSCH, *the Michael's Café bartender,*
remembers the last time she saw John Unitas:

John was here the day that he passed away. He had lunch here and then said he was going to work out, which was his usual routine. It wasn't that much later that we got the call that he had passed away. His daughter's best friend was sitting at the end of the bar, when the call came in. That's how we heard all about it.

John's favorite thing to eat here was the crab cakes. He had those almost every time he came here. He had had a little bit of an episode with his heart about a year and a half earlier (Unitas had also had an emergency bypass in the early nineties), and he knew he needed to be careful. He usually ate well. That day he had the liver and a side of mashed potatoes. That really wasn't that good for him, but he loved it.

We used to joke. I would say to him, "I'm going to be working until I drop," and he goes, "So will I." He certainly was.

RICHARD SAMMIS:

On the day he passed away, John was here, at his office, from 9:30 to 2:30. He had already been to lunch. That day we laughed and we talked and we put some golf dates in our appointment books. He was perfect: he had no aches, he had no pains. He was fine.

He came out of his office at around 2:30 and started to walk up those steps (to the ground floor), and I could hear him whistling, because he always whistled. He stopped, turned back around, and came back downstairs. "Tricky." He used to call me Tricky. "Hey, Tricky, I'm going to go work out and then go home. " I said, "John, are you coming in in the morning." And he said, "Absolutely." I said, "Be careful. I'll see you early in the morning. Bring the coffee." He said, "Okay, I'll bring the coffee."

John walked up those steps, got into his car, drove about eight and a half minutes around to the workout place on Timonium Road, went inside, changed his clothes, came out, saw the doctor, told him a joke, they both laughed. The doctor then went one way and John went the other way, and within two steps the doctor heard John hit the floor. They had a defibrillator there, they had a heart doctor there, and John was dead before he hit the ground. That's how fast it was.

Then people started calling me and I said, "You're crazy! He just left here." But it was true. I was so sad after it first happened, but I've gotten to where I can look back and appreciate my having a twenty-five-year relationship with a man like him. When I close my eyes, I can still see him. I was so lucky to be with him for those years.

Johnny Unitas, perhaps the greatest quarterback who ever lived.

JOHN UNITAS'S CAREER NFL STATISTICS

Year	Team	W-L	Comp.	Att.	Pct.	Yds.	TDs	Int.
1956	Baltimore Colts	5–7	110	198	55.6	1,498	9	10
1957	Baltimore Colts	7–5	172	301	57.1	2,550	24	17
1958	Baltimore Colts	9–3	136	263	51.7	2,007	19	7
1959	Baltimore Colts	9–3	193	367	52.6	2,899	32	14
1960	Baltimore Colts	6–6	190	378	50.3	3,099	25	24
1961	Baltimore Colts	8–6	229	420	54.5	2,990	16	24
1962	Baltimore Colts	7–7	222	389	57.1	2,967	23	23
1963	Baltimore Colts	8–6	237	410	57.8	3,481	20	12
1964	Baltimore Colts	12–2	158	305	51.8	2,824	19	6
1965	Baltimore Colts	10–3–1	164	282	58.2	2,530	23	12
1966	Baltimore Colts	9–5	195	348	56.0	2,748	22	24
1967	Baltimore Colts	11–1–2	255	436	58.5	3,428	20	16
1968	Baltimore Colts	13–1	11	32	34.4	139	2	4
1969	Baltimore Colts	8–5–1	178	327	54.4	2,342	12	20
1970	Baltimore Colts	11–2–1	166	321	51.7	2,213	14	18
1971	Baltimore Colts	10–4	92	176	52.3	942	3	9
1972	Baltimore Colts	5–9	88	157	56.1	1,111	4	6
1973	San Diego Chargers	2–11–1	34	76	44.7	471	3	7
TOTAL			2,830	5,186	54.6	40,239	290	253

SOURCE: 2002 Indianapolis Colts Media Guide and Baltimore Sun

JOHNNY UNITAS'S 47-GAME STREAK WITH AT LEAST ONE TOUCHDOWN PASS

No.	Date	Opponent	Site	Result	Comp.	Att.	Yds.	TDs	Ints.
				1956					
1.	Dec. 9	Los Angeles	Away	L, 7–31	14	29	147	1	1
	• 3 yards to Jim Mutscheller								
2.	Dec. 16	San Francisco	Away	L, 17–30	11	16	124	1	1
	• 31 yards to Raymond Berry								
3.	Dec. 23	Washington	Home	W, 19–17	10	18	161	1	1
	• 53 yards to Jim Mutscheller								
				1957					
4.	Sept. 29	Detroit	Home	W, 34–14	14	23	241	4	3
	• 44 yards to Jim Mutscheller								
	• 35 yards to L. G. Dupre								
	• 35 yards to Raymond Berry								
	• 3 yards to L. G. Dupre								

SOURCE: 2002 Indianapolis Colts Media Guide, Baltimore Sun
NOTES: 1. Unitas missed two games in November 1958 because of bruised ribs.
2. The streak ended December 11 at Los Angeles against the Rams.

No.	Date	Opponent	Site	Result	Comp.	Att.	Yds.	TDs	Ints.
5.	Oct. 5	Chicago	Home	W, 20–10	17	26	184	2	1

- 8 yards to Jim Mutscheller
- 9 yards to Alan Ameche

No.	Date	Opponent	Site	Result	Comp.	Att.	Yds.	TDs	Ints.
6.	Oct. 13	Green Bay	Away	W, 45–17	7	17	130	2	2

- 12 yards to Jim Mutscheller
- 29 yards to Jim Mutscheller

No.	Date	Opponent	Site	Result	Comp.	Att.	Yds.	TDs	Ints.
7.	Oct. 20	Detroit	Away	L, 27–31	16	21	239	4	1

- 15 yards to Jim Mutscheller
- 72 yards to Lenny Moore
- 52 yards to Jim Mutscheller
- 4 yards to Lenny Moore

No.	Date	Opponent	Site	Result	Comp.	Att.	Yds.	TDs	Ints.
8.	Oct. 27	Green Bay	Home	L, 21–24	16	31	188	2	2

- 52 yards to Raymond Berry
- 6 yards to Lenny Moore

No.	Date	Opponent	Site	Result	Comp.	Att.	Yds.	TDs	Ints.
9.	Nov. 3	Pittsburgh	Home	L, 13–19	9	3	56	1	3

- 5 yards to Raymond Berry

No.	Date	Opponent	Site	Result	Comp.	Att.	Yds.	TDs	Ints.
10.	Nov. 10	Washington	Away	W, 21–17	17	30	247	2	0

- 67 yards to Raymond Berry
- 11 yards to Raymond Berry

No.	Date	Opponent	Site	Result	Comp.	Att.	Yds.	TDs	Ints.
11.	Nov. 17	Chicago	Away	W, 29–14	11	23	245	1	0

- 66 yards to Jim Mutscheller

No.	Date	Opponent	Site	Result	Comp.	Att.	Yds.	TDs	Ints.
12.	Nov. 24	San Francisco	Home	W, 27–21	16	25	230	1	0

- 8 yards to Alan Ameche

No.	Date	Opponent	Site	Result	Comp.	Att.	Yds.	TDs	Ints.
13.	Dec. 1	Los Angeles	Home	W, 31–14	18	30	271	3	1

- 3 yards to Lenny Moore
- 10 yards to Raymond Berry
- 50 yards to Lenny Moore

No.	Date	Opponent	Site	Result	Comp.	Att.	Yds.	TDs	Ints.
14.	Dec. 8	San Francisco	Away	L, 13–17	23	37	296	1	2

- 82 yards to Lenny Moore

No.	Date	Opponent	Site	Result	Comp.	Att.	Yds.	TDs	Ints.
15.	Dec. 15	Los Angeles	Away	L, 21–37	14	29	223	1	2

- 2 yards to Lenny Moore

No.	Date	Opponent	Site	Result	Comp.	Att.	Yds.	TDs	Ints.

1958

No.	Date	Opponent	Site	Result	Comp.	Att.	Yds.	TDs	Ints.
16.	Sept. 28	Detroit	Home	W, 28–15	23	43	250	2	1

• 26 yards to Raymond Berry
• 14 yards to Raymond Berry

No.	Date	Opponent	Site	Result	Comp.	Att.	Yds.	TDs	Ints.
17.	Oct. 4	Chicago	Home	W, 51–38	10	23	198	4	1

• 12 yards to Raymond Berry
• 77 yards to Lenny Moore
• 2 yards to Jim Mutscheller
• 33 yards to Lenny Moore

No.	Date	Opponent	Site	Result	Comp.	Att.	Yds.	TDs	Ints.
18.	Oct. 12	Green Bay	Away	W, 24–17	16	35	238	1	1

• 54 yards to Jim Mutscheller

No.	Date	Opponent	Site	Result	Comp.	Att.	Yds.	TDs	Ints.
19.	Oct. 19	Detroit	Away	W, 40–14	11	17	221	1	0

• 37 yards to Jim Mutscheller

No.	Date	Opponent	Site	Result	Comp.	Att.	Yds.	TDs	Ints.
20.	Oct. 26	Washington	Home	W, 35–10	8	15	183	2	0

• 17 yards to Raymond Berry
• 48 yards to Raymond Berry

No.	Date	Opponent	Site	Result	Comp.	Att.	Yds.	TDs	Ints.
21.	Nov. 2	Green Bay	Home	W, 56–0	5	16	99	2	0

• 2 yards to Lenny Moore
• 5 yards to Alan Ameche

No.	Date	Opponent	Site	Result	Comp.	Att.	Yds.	TDs	Ints.
22.	Nov. 23	Los Angeles	Home	W, 34–7	12	18	218	2	0

• 58 yards to Lenny Moore
• 12 yards to Jim Mutscheller

No.	Date	Opponent	Site	Result	Comp.	Att.	Yds.	TDs	Ints.
23.	Nov. 30	San Francisco	Home	W, 35–27	17	33	229	1	1

• 7 yards to Raymond Berry

No.	Date	Opponent	Site	Result	Comp.	Att.	Yds.	TDs	Ints.
24.	Dec. 6	Los Angeles	Away	L, 28–30	23	38	214	3	3

• 3 yards to Raymond Berry
• 5 yards to Lenny Moore
• 22 yards to Jim Mutscheller

No.	Date	Opponent	Site	Result	Comp.	Att.	Yds.	TDs	Ints.
25.	Dec. 14	San Francisco	Away,	L, 12–21	11	25	157	1	0

• 38 yards to Jim Mutscheller

No.	Date	Opponent	Site	Result	Comp.	Att.	Yds.	TDs	Ints.
				1959					
26.	Sept. 27	Detroit	Home	W, 21–9	13	30	230	2	0

• 18 yards to Raymond Berry
• 40 yards to Jim Mutscheller

| 27. | Oct. 3 | Chicago | Home | L, 21–26 | 17 | 38 | 221 | 3 | 3 |

• 7 yards to Raymond Berry
• 4 yards to Jim Mutscheller
• 13 yards to Jim Mutscheller

| 28. | Oct. 11 | Detroit | Away | W, 31–24 | 13 | 25 | 257 | 3 | 2 |

• 68 yards to Lenny Moore
• 39 yards to Jim Mutscheller
• 53 yards to Raymond Berry

| 29. | Oct. 18 | Chicago | Away | W, 21–7 | 16 | 30 | 233 | 2 | 2 |

• 25 yards to Lenny Moore
• 1 yard to L. G. Dupre

| 30. | Oct. 25 | Green Bay | Home | W, 38–21 | 19 | 29 | 206 | 3 | 0 |

• 8 yards to Raymond Berry
• 3 yards to Alan Ameche
• 2 yards to Raymond Berry

| 31. | Nov. 1 | Cleveland | Home | L, 31–38 | 23 | 41 | 397 | 4 | 3 |

• 3 yards to Lenny Moore
• 8 yards to Jerry Richardson
• 10 yards to Raymond Berry
• 5 yards to Jim Mutscheller

| 32. | Nov. 8 | Washington | Away | L, 24–27 | 15 | 35 | 265 | 2 | 2 |

• 19 yards to Jim Mutscheller
• 4 yards to Jim Mutscheller

| 33. | Nov. 15 | Green Bay | Away | W, 28–24 | 19 | 33 | 324 | 3 | 0 |

• 7 yards to Raymond Berry
• 10 yards to Raymond Berry
• 24 yards to Jim Mutscheller

No.	Date	Opponent	Site	Result	Comp.	Att.	Yds.	TDs	Ints.
34.	Nov. 22	San Francisco	Home	W, 45—14	10	19	141	2	1

• 12 yards to Raymond Berry
• 3 yards to Lenny Moore

35.	Nov. 29	Los Angeles	Home	W, 35—21	14	24	242	2	1

• 55 yards to Raymond Berry
• 17 yards to Lenny Moore

36.	Dec. 5	San Francisco	Away	W, 34—14	21	36	273	3	0

• 7 yards to Raymond Berry
• 13 yards to Raymond Berry
• 64 yards to Lenny Moore

37.	Dec. 12	Los Angeles	Away	W, 45—26	13	27	110	3	0

• 7 yards to Raymond Berry
• 11 yards to Raymond Berry
• 9 yards to Jerry Richardson

1960

38.	Sept. 25	Washington	Home	W, 20—0	17	35	232	1	1

• 12 yards to Raymond Berry

39.	Oct. 2	Chicago	Home	W, 42—7	14	27	307	4	0

• 66 yards to Lenny Moore
• 27 yards to Raymond Berry
• 18 yards to Lenny Moore
• 43 yards to Jim Mutscheller

40.	Oct. 9	Green Bay	Away	L, 21—35	16	31	216	1	4

• 1 yard to Alex Hawkins

41.	Oct. 16	Los Angeles	Home	W, 31—17	12	23	176	1	2

• 22 yards to Lenny Moore

42.	Oct. 23	Detroit	Away	L, 17—30	20	40	253	2	2

• 22 yards to Raymond Berry
• 2 yards to Jim Mutscheller

No.	Date	Opponent	Site	Result	Comp.	Att.	Yds.	TDs	Ints.
43.	Oct. 30	Dallas	Away	W, 45–7	8	16	270	4	0
	• 68 yards to Raymond Berry								
	• 52 yards to Raymond Berry								
	• 70 yards to Raymond Berry								
	• 20 yards to Lenny Moore								
44.	Nov. 6	Green Bay	Home	W, 38–24	20	29	324	4	1
	• 45 yards to Raymond Berry								
	• 1 yard to Alex Hawkins								
	• 21 yards to Raymond Berry								
	• 16 yards to Raymond Berry								
45.	Nov. 13	Chicago	Away	W, 24–20	16	33	266	2	2
	• 36 yards to Lenny Moore								
	• 39 yards to Lenny Moore								
46.	Nov. 27	San Francisco	Home	L, 22–30	16	30	356	3	5
	• 10 yards to Raymond Berry								
	• 6 yards to Alex Hawkins								
	• 65 yards to Lenny Moore								
47.	Dec. 4	Detroit	Home	L, 15–20	22	40	357	2	3
	• 80 yards to Lenny Moore								
	• 39 yards to Lenny Moore								

Notes

Chapter 1: Steel Town

1. *Baltimore Sun*, October 20, 2002.
2. Ibid.
3. Ibid.
4. Ibid.
5. Ibid.

Chapter 2: Bluegrass and Sandlots

1. University of Louisville Sports Information Department archives, 1980 interview.
2. *Baltimore Sun*, October 20, 2002.
3. Ibid.
4. University of Louisville football media guide.
5. Zimmerman, Paul, *The New Thinking Man's Guide to Pro Football*. New York: Simon and Schuster, 1984, 72.
6. *Baltimore Sun*, October 20, 2002.
7. Ibid.
8. Ibid.

9. Ibid.

10. Gildea, William, *When the Colts Belonged to Baltimore*. New York: Ticknor and Fields, 1994, 174.

11. Schaap, Dick, *Quarterbacks Have All the Fun*. Chicago, IL: Playboy Press, 1974, 13.

Chapter 3: The Baltimore Colts

1. Gildea, William, *When the Colts Belonged to Baltimore*. New York: Ticknor and Fields, 1994, 181–182.

2. Ibid., 129–130.

3. *Baltimore Sun*, October 20, 2002.

4. Shula, Don, and Lou Sahadi, *The Winning Edge*. New York: E. P. Dutton, 1973, 100.

5. Ibid., 99–101.

6. Hawkins, Alex, *Then Came Brain Damage*. Marietta, GA: Longstreet Press, 1991, 66.

Chapter 4: Johnny U

1. *Baltimore Sun*, October 20, 2002.

2. Gildea, William, *When the Colts Belonged to Baltimore*. New York: Ticknor and Fields, 1994, 209.

3. Zimmerman, Paul, *The New Thinking Man's Guide to Pro Football*. New York: Simon and Schuster, 1984, 59.

4. *Sports Illustrated*, September 23, 2002.

5. *USA Today*, September 12, 2002.

6. Ibid.

7. *Sports Illustrated*, September 23, 2002.

8. Hawkins, Alex, *My Story (And I'm Sticking to It)*. Chapel Hill, NC: Algonquin Books of Chapel Hill, 1990, 108.

9. Rosenthal, Harold, *Fifty Faces of Football*. New York: Athenum, 1981, 200.

10. Gildea, William, *When the Colts Belonged to Baltimore*. New York: Ticknor and Fields, 1994, 207–208.

11. Ibid., 204.

12. Schaap, Dick, *Quarterbacks have All the Fun*. Chicago, IL: Playboy Press, 1974, 8–9.

13. Ibid., 5.
14. Zimmerman, Paul, *The New Thinking Man's Guide to Pro Football*. New York: Simon and Schuster, 1984, 67.
15. *Sports Illustrated*, September 23, 2002.
16. *The Sporting News*, September 18–24, 2002.
17. Hawkins, Alex, *My Story (And I'm Sticking to It)*. Chapel Hill, NC: Algonquin Books of Chapel Hill, 1990, 88–89.
18. Ibid., 4.
19. ESPN.com, Sept. 12, 2002.
20. Rosenthal, Harold, *Fifty Faces of Football*. New York: Athenum, 1981, 202.
21. *Baltimore Sun*, October 20, 2002.
22. Zimmerman, Paul, *The New Thinking Man's Guide to Pro Football*. New York: Simon and Schuster, 1984, 80.
23. *Sports Illustrated*, September 23, 2002.
24. *The Sporting News*, September 18–24, 2002.

Chapter 5: Unitas We Stand

1. Schachter, Norm, *Close Calls*. New York: William Morrow and Company, 1981, 77–78.
2. Ibid., 105–06.
3. *The Sporting News*, September 18–24, 2002.
4. Ibid.
5. *USA Today*, September 12, 2002.
6. Hawkins, Alex, *My Story (And I'm Sticking to It)*. Chapel Hill, NC: Algonquin Books of Chapel Hill, 1990, 137.
7. *Baltimore Sun*, October 20, 2002.
8. Gildea, William, *When the Colts Belonged to Baltimore*. New York: Ticknor and Fields, 1994, 205.
9. *Baltimore Sun*, October 20, 2002.
10. *The Sporting News*, September 18–24, 2002.
11. Hawkins, Alex, *My Story (And I'm Sticking to It)*. Chapel Hill, NC: Algonquin Books of Chapel Hill, 1990, 105.
12. *Baltimore Sun*, October 20, 2002.

INDEX